CW00346327

THE MATURITY OF

THE MATURITY OF BELIEF

Critically Assessing Religious Faith

Kevin Twain Lowery

continuum

Published by Continuum
The Tower Building   80 Maiden Lane
11 York Road   Suite 704
London SE1 7NX   New York, NY 10038

www.continuumbooks.com

British Library Cataloguing-in-Publication Data
A catalogue record for this book is available from the British Library

ISBN-10: HB: 0-8264-9853-1
PB: 0-8264-9854-X
ISBN-13: HB: 978-0-8264-9853-3
PB: 978-0-8264-9854-0

Typeset by Servis Filmsetting Ltd, Manchester
Printed on acid-free paper in Great Britain by
Athenaeum Press Ltd, Gateshead, Tyne and Wear

To Amy

CONTENTS

CONTENTS

INTRODUCTION

Religion is drawing much criticism in the world today. Conflict between religious groups is certainly not a new or recent development, because religion has been a source of contention throughout human history. However, a growing number of voices are calling attention to the problems caused by religious fanaticism. Some feel that the solution lies in 'experiencing God', uniting people through mystical religious encounters. This is extremely naive, since mysticism is as old as religion itself and has seldom (if ever) had a unifying effect beyond a particular circle of people. Instead, mystical experience typically polarizes those that have these experiences from those who do not. These experiences can be either helpful or harmful, depending upon the beliefs of the people who have them. The experiences merely confirm the beliefs that they hold. Those who hate their enemies have mystical experiences, as do those who love their enemies. These experiences are often interpreted as the imprimatur of God. Consequently, the real problem is not religious experience, but religious belief, and therein lies the real solution. Beliefs must have a much better basis than mystical experience.

Among those who recognize religious belief as the source of difficulty, many will readily offer pluralism as the cure for religious hostility. After all, we would no longer need to feel threatened by the beliefs of others if we could somehow validate all religious beliefs in some way. In reality, this proposal seeks to avoid the true problem rather than to address it squarely. Perhaps the desire to affirm all religious beliefs stems from a spirit of benevolence, or it may also be motivated by a desire to protect one's own religious beliefs, and this cannot be done without protecting religious belief in general. I suspect that a growing number of people fear that their own religious beliefs may not withstand the scrutiny that they would impose on the religious beliefs of others, and it is easier to affirm all religious belief. Nevertheless, pluralism must also be understood in its postmodern context as a desire to render all truth claims as wholly subjective. I shall argue that this is an overreaction to those who claim absolute certainty for their beliefs.

Of course, the term 'pluralism' is also used to denote an attitude of tolerance, and I am very supportive of this. I believe that this can be cultivated without endorsing pluralism according to the stronger usage of the term, i.e. the claim that all religions are equally valid. (In this book I will be using the term 'pluralism' according to this stronger usage.) The key to promoting religious tolerance without endorsing pluralism is found in the maturity of religious belief. Indeed, it is not necessary to be a pluralist in order to recognize the fact that there is some truth in all religions. Only the most sectarian religious groups deny this. However, in consideration of the discrepancies that exist between the many religions that have ever existed, it seems that if pluralism were true, we would have to conclude that God is rather ineffective and incompetent in choosing ways to be revealed in the world. In that regard, pluralism seems less feasible than Deism (the belief that God created the world but does not interact with it at all), because pluralism makes stronger claims that are more difficult to substantiate.

A number of the critics blame religion for many of the world's problems throughout history. They argue that religion needs to be eliminated altogether. To start, this is quixotic, because human beings have consistently demonstrated an impulse towards religious belief, and there is little reason to believe that it could be supplanted any time soon, if ever. It only seems natural to speculate about the realm of the unknown – to wonder about the ultimate nature of reality. All in all, I feel that the call to eliminate religion is another overreaction to religious fanaticism. Extreme often begets extreme. People tend to polarize toward the extremes, because it is easier to support one side of the argument and flatly dismiss other viewpoints than it is to evaluate, prioritize, and hold all of the competing claims in tension with one another. When we are exposed to an extreme position, we will either find it appealing or appalling. Consequently, we will be tempted either to adopt that position in our own thinking or to react strongly against it by championing an opposite extreme.

The problem is not religious belief per se, but the immaturity with which the beliefs are held. We start forming beliefs at a very early age, and the process continues throughout our lives. The concepts that we construct as children are fairly simple, and this simplicity represents the limitations of our ability to reason. As we grow and mature, we begin to see complexities that were previously hidden from us, and our concepts consequently become more sophisticated. It stands to reason that our maturity is dependent upon the maturity of our thinking. This maxim holds true not only for individuals, but also for humanity in general. For example, past generations held simplistic beliefs such as these: 1) the earth is at the centre of the universe; 2) epileptics are demon-possessed; and 3) the king speaks on behalf of the gods, so his words cannot be rescinded. As humanity progressed, these beliefs were eventually rejected, and they were replaced with beliefs that reflect a greater level of intellectual maturity. We consider these changes to be real progress, because the new beliefs are more reliable and are thus probably truer than the previous beliefs. The gains of such changes far outweigh the losses.

Consequently, it is more valid to argue that particular *kinds* of religious belief should be eliminated, not religious belief in general. In writing this book, my goal is indeed to encourage people to move beyond simplistic religious concepts and to mature in their thinking. We do not need to feel threatened by those who do not share our beliefs. The more our thinking matures, the more confident we will feel with our beliefs, because we will have better reasons for holding them. At the same time, we will also realize the fallibility of our beliefs, determined by the limitations of our thinking. This tempers our confidence with a feeling of humility. Confidence and humility are two of the more notable fruits of mature thinking. Although many people try to exhibit them, they only come to full fruition through intellectual maturity, and this must be achieved gradually, not in one huge step. The process is very important and cannot be truncated.

This book focuses on the nature of belief itself, not on particular beliefs per se. Consequently, this book should be appropriate for readers at various levels of intellectual maturity. In fact, there are many people who are otherwise mature and sophisticated thinkers who are still encumbered with simplistic religious beliefs, and this prevents them from enjoying the maturity and sophistication of which they are more than capable. This may be due in part to a lack of exposure, but it is hoped that every person would want to learn and mature, because this is how real and lasting growth takes place.

My own thinking has been greatly spurred by the philosophy of Immanuel Kant. In his *Prolegomena to Any Future Metaphysics*, Kant confesses that the writings of David Hume awakened him from his dogmatic slumber. Reading Kant had essentially the same effect on me in graduate school. As a result, part of the inspiration for this book comes from three of Kant's works. First, his essay 'What Is Enlightenment?' argues that intellectual maturity is being able to think for oneself. Unfortunately, too many people are satisfied to live in a perpetual state of immaturity and allow others to think for them. Second, Kant's great work *Religion within the Boundaries of Reason Alone* seeks to determine the proper limits of metaphysics, especially religious belief. In that book Kant also argues that the real basis of religion is morality. That particular thesis will be the focus of my next project. This book will remain centred on the epistemic limits of religious beliefs. Third, Kant wrote *Conflict of the Faculties* towards the end of his life, and this offers a critique of the relationship between theology and other academic disciplines that is still relevant today.

This book is divided into four major sections. Section One sets the stage by introducing the main thesis of the book. The task of the first chapter is to examine the function of belief and the way that beliefs are formed and interrelated. Chapter two explores some common reasons why many people prefer simplistic thinking to intellectual maturity, especially in their religious beliefs. A case is made for moving beyond simplistic concepts and embracing more sophisticated ones. Although a number of epistemological issues surface in these early chapters, the discussion is not technical. Rather, the purpose is to probe belief in a more general sense, and this emphasis is maintained throughout the book.

The second section of the book is an exposition of general trends in Western intellectual history. It serves as a background for the rest of the book, and it underscores the fact that certain types of religious belief revert to antiquated ways of thinking. Chapter 3 looks at the characteristics of religious belief before the Enlightenment, and Chapter 4 centres on the early part of the Enlightenment, starting with Descartes. The impact of Kant and his successors is traced in the fifth chapter, and the sixth chapter looks at developments which followed the modern period from the middle of the nineteenth century through the twentieth century. In the end, I advocate a healthy level of scepticism, one that embraces epistemic fallibility and humility, but not to the extent of precluding all belief and knowledge. Rather, there must be an ongoing desire to pursue truth and objectivity as much as our epistemic limits will allow.

In Section Three, the discussion returns to the dynamics of belief, especially those that are particular to religious belief. Chapter 7 aims at determining what is a proper basis for belief. I conclude that it is best to evaluate beliefs according to their reliability, and this process is then explored. The eighth chapter considers the interrelatedness of beliefs and the impact that this has on the formation and replacement of beliefs. In Chapter 9 attention is given to analysing the sources of religious belief with regard to their interdependence and limitations, indicating the weight that they should be given.

The final section of the book more fully describes the characteristics of mature religious belief, then it points towards the path to intellectual maturity. In Chapter 10, the discussion focuses on the quest for certainty. Here the mediated position of moderate scepticism I am advocating is expanded in terms of certainty and doubt. The eleventh chapter uses the preceding discussion of certainty and doubt to inform the way that faith is conceived and regarded as mature. The book ends with Chapter 12, which provides some guidelines for fostering intellectual maturity in our religious beliefs.

One of the difficulties of undertaking a book such as this is that it may not appeal to those who can perhaps benefit from it most. I have in mind those who have intentionally stopped growing intellectually with regard to their religious beliefs, choosing to remain on a plateau of some sort. This is not to suggest that their religious faith has grown stale or dull; they may enjoy things the way they are. In fact, many people want to keep their faith simple precisely in order to preserve their feelings. They are afraid of moving beyond the stage of innocence, the place where concerns and worries are minimized, where problems and difficulties are either ignored or oversimplified. More importantly, the stage of innocence is a safe haven for cherished beliefs, because beliefs in this stage are not tested or challenged in any significant way. In effect, these people are afraid to allow their religious beliefs to mature intellectually, because this will undermine, if not destroy, the happiness that they derive from them.

This is the equivalent of a husband and wife who try to keep their marriage in the 'honeymoon stage'. They intentionally refuse to allow their relationship to mature, because they will have to give up their idealizations and learn to love one another for who they really are. This reminds me of a particular part of my childhood. As a boy believing in Santa Claus, Christmas was always thrilling, for it was shrouded with a sense of mystery and eager anticipation. For several years, my mother feared that my excitement for Christmas would be lost should I cease to believe in old St Nick. Of course, I eventually relinquished my belief in Santa Claus, and although a certain inno- cent fascination with Christmas was lost, it was soon displaced by a much deeper appreciation. I began to realize the sacrifices that my parents made in order to make Christmas special for my brother and me. This sense of appreciation only grew and intensified as I assumed the role of a parent, making the same kind of sacrifices for my children. In the same way, although a certain religious exuber- ance may be lost in the process of maturing, it can be replaced with deeper levels of appreciation and satisfaction.

In this book I will attempt to discuss religious belief as broadly as possible. However, since my own religious background is rooted in Christianity, I have much more familiarity with that tradition than I do with other perspectives. Although the discussion will at times be predominantly Christian, I believe that the principles discussed can be applied more generally to other religions and to other disciplines of knowledge. I am convinced that the ancient philosophers were right in claiming that happiness, virtue and truth are all intertwined. It seems to me that happiness of the deepest sort is only found in a life devoted to true virtue and a genuine pursuit of truth. It is my hope that this book will be of use to many in the pursuit of truth and hence lead to a greater understanding of virtue and happiness as well.

SECTION ONE

HOW AND WHY WE BELIEVE

CHAPTER 1

THE NATURE OF BELIEF

MAKING SENSE OF REALITY

From our earliest moments, we gather information from the world around us. Even before we are born, we begin to experience sensations of various sorts. When we finally leave the safe confines of the womb, we enter a world where we are continually bombarded with data that we collect through our senses. It is staggering to try to imagine the amount of information a person takes in during the course of a lifetime. In order to make sense of this information, we must interpret the experiences we have. In essence, we relate bits of information to one another, organizing them into some type of order. Without this process, our experiences are insignificant, because it is only after we interpret experience that it becomes personally meaningful to us.

Think of how a young child comes to understand the meaning of a simple sentence like 'Bring me the red ball.' A ball is in a general sense a round object, so the concept of 'ball' is derived from a prior concept of 'roundness' that the child must have already learned. (This is different from a child merely memorizing words to represent specific objects.) However, there are many round objects that we would not want the child to attempt to carry, and even some of these are designated as some type of ball (e.g. cheese ball, meatball, bowling ball). Requesting a 'red' ball limits the possibilities and helps the child determine the precise nature of the request, and yet it is most likely that the child identifies the specific ball that has been requested from the context of the statement. (Asking for *the* red ball, and not *a* red ball, indicates that I have a specific ball in mind.) It would be relatively safe to assume either that the child often plays with a particular red ball or that a particular red ball is within plain view. Of course, the child must also have attached meaning to the words 'bring' and 'me' before the request will be intelligible, but the general point is made.

This basic example helps to illustrate the way that we form concepts from our basic sensations and perceptions. In so doing, we essentially interpret our sensations and perceptions, attaching meaning to them. Now let us consider another example that is more complex yet still familiar. Imagine that you are in a town or city, walking to your car late at night. All of a sudden, you feel something poking you in the back. This sensation has no explicit meaning for you until you interpret it. Perhaps the feeling is caused by a physical condition, indicating a health problem. However, given the situation, you might suspect that some unfamiliar or unfriendly person is behind you, maybe a mugger. A sense of uneasiness (perhaps fear) sweeps over you, but then you hear familiar laughter, and you turn to discover one of your friends playing a joke on you. Within a few short moments the experience is reinterpreted and given new meaning. Even then, you may or may not appreciate your friend's sense of humour, so it is not apparent that this would end up being a positive experience for everyone.

The process of assimilating information is what leads to the formation of beliefs. In general, we form beliefs as we attempt to make sense of reality, as we interpret life's experiences. More specifically, our beliefs are based upon the perceptions we have of ourselves, our own well-being, and the world around us. For instance, a young woman in the situation given above may initially believe that she is in immediate danger, and this would indicate that she perceives a real threat to her well-being. However, we can also envision various scenarios where she would not necessarily feel endangered: for instance, she might be an expert in martial arts, a law enforcement officer, or someone otherwise specially trained in self-defence, and this could give her confidence in her ability to escape this predicament – she may even relish the opportunity to sharpen her skills in a real-life situation.

Even perceptions themselves can be regarded as a fundamental form of belief. Perceptions differ from mere sensation, because a perception is only formed once we come to some type of conclusion about the sensations we experience. If I hear a sound, I know only that I have heard something until I form a belief as to what that sound might be. Once I reach a conclusion about the sensation,

I form a perception about it. We typically follow this process in forming our beliefs. Hence, belief is generally grounded in empirical (i.e. sensory) experience. Our memories and self-awareness are also critical sources in belief formation, but these are likewise dependent upon empirical experience. When we form metaphysical beliefs (about God, the afterlife, etc.), we must abstract these concepts from empirical ones. Thomas Aquinas understood this, explaining that we can only speak of God through the use of analogy. The same is true of all metaphysical belief.

Our most basic beliefs are formed at a very early age, and we subsequently use existing beliefs to form new beliefs. In other words, we do not 'reinvent the wheel', so to speak, every time we form a new belief. Rather, we build upon the beliefs that we already have, synthesizing existing beliefs with one another and with new information that we have gathered. As a result, beliefs are interdependent. That is why our general belief structure is sometimes referred to as the 'web of belief'. When one of our beliefs is altered in some way, other beliefs must also be altered if the overall structure is to remain coherent. Of course, some of our beliefs are more crucial than others in the overall belief structure, and they thus affect a greater number of beliefs.

The interdependence of beliefs makes epistemic integrity all the more important. If one belief is unreliable, then other beliefs are likely to be unreliable as well. In order to ensure the reliability of beliefs, some choose to limit belief to that which can be verified by empirical experience alone. Unfortunately, this considerably limits the meaning that we can attach to life's experiences, and many of us are not satisfied with this restriction. We want to believe that events have a meaning that is deeper than that which we subjectively attach to it. This is where religious belief (and metaphysical belief in general) becomes relevant. In the broadest sense of the word, religion includes our beliefs about what is ultimately meaningful. Consequently, not only are our religious beliefs focused on the sacred, but the beliefs are themselves regarded as sacred. Religion thus gives us a broader framework for interpreting life's experiences, especially with regard to circumstances which are beyond our control. It serves an important psychological function, one that should be neither denied nor ignored, because it greatly influences the way we interpret the events of our lives.

Nevertheless, for many people religious belief offers little consolation if it is merely subjective, being nothing more than a psychological coping mechanism. In order for it to be truly useful, it must point to some ultimate reality, one which transcends the limits of our existence and gives us a basis for faith and hope. It must give us reason to believe in something greater than ourselves and the world in which we live. Like many religions, this is certainly the case with Christianity, which has historically asserted that there is in reality a God who is revealed to us, both in history and through personal encounter. Christianity is thus premised upon belief in a metaphysical (i.e. spiritual) reality. As a result, Christianity makes claims about an objective, ultimate reality that transcends our empirical experience.

However, the empirical realm is precisely where we are able to perceive things with a higher level of objectivity. In other words, we generally trust our senses enough to presuppose that what we perceive through them is reliable. Common experience tells us that this trust is well placed, because other people perceive things empirically in a manner that is consistent with the way that we perceive them. If I see a thunderstorm approaching, I have a strong basis for believing that other people will also see the thunderstorm approaching. Hence, my observation has a high degree of objectivity and reliability. To the extent that my beliefs have an empirical basis, I can generally regard them as objective and reliable.

Since religious belief goes beyond the realm of the empirical, it is by nature highly subjective. In essence, although I may believe in an ultimate, objective reality, the *basis* for that belief is not necessarily objective. In other words, the act of believing in something objective is not itself objective. The basis for the belief is what determines its objectivity and subjectivity. In short, the subjectivity of religious belief makes it less reliable than empirically based belief. However, there are other ways to establish reliability, as we shall see.

THE DESIRE TO BELIEVE

I would argue that, under normal circumstances, a person of sound mind will not be utterly indifferent to belief. Even naiveté and scepticism are both based upon more fundamental beliefs. The naive person believes that many beliefs can be trusted, and the sceptic believes that few beliefs can be trusted. A person's willingness or unwillingness to trust will itself be a conglomerate of more basic beliefs, constructed from one's life experiences. If trust is rewarded, then it will be reinforced, but if it is punished or not rewarded, then it will be undermined and the person will defensively avoid reliving the pain of misplaced trust.

Belief is the means through which we find meaning in life. Without it, life seems pointless. Even Nietzsche, who advocated a type of nihilism, did not reject meaning altogether. Rather, he claimed that the only thing of real worth is oneself, and so the term *ubërmensch* (the 'over-man'/'superman') applies to those who assert themselves against the 'herd' of society. The point is this: even if some people conclude that life has no meaning, this does not suggest that they delight in this conclusion. We all naturally want to promote our own well-being and happiness. Kant said that pursuing one's own happiness thus cannot be a moral duty, because we all do it anyway. Jonathan Edwards likewise felt that we all naturally care about our own well-being, and this is what we essentially refer to as 'self-love', a natural part of the human psyche. Indeed, we generally regard a lack of concern for one's own well-being as a form of psychosis, because it is not natural to the healthy individual.

Fortunately, we are able to value things beyond our own narrow self-interest. We are able to decide that some things are more important than our own immediate well-being and happiness. Otherwise, there would be no such thing as sacrifice, because all would be done for one's own sake alone. We thus can hold beliefs that cover a range of values that is broader than our own self-interest. I would like to think that all of our beliefs are valued to some extent, because they have some usefulness to us. Most of us know or believe things that we would consider to be trivial, but perhaps our ability to learn trivia may itself be considered beneficial.

Nevertheless, our beliefs cover an array of matters, and each one has its own type and degree of importance to us. The more important a certain matter is to us, the more important its corresponding beliefs will be to us. In fact, you can often tell what people care about most by identifying the beliefs that they value the most. This is why many people find it difficult to discuss topics like religion, ethics and politics. However, identifying what people care deeply about does not necessarily indicate *why* they care about it deeply.

It should be pointed out that rejecting a belief does not indicate indifference to it. Just as we can believe things either strongly or weakly, we can also reject things strongly or weakly. In fact, rejecting something is itself a belief. Rather than believe that something is true, we believe that it is false. We reject the proposition and accept its negation. However, we can also suspend judgement on a matter if we feel that there is insufficient evidence to come to a conclusion. The fact remains that the more important a particular belief is to us, the more we will care about it, regardless of whether we accept it, reject it, or remain undecided.

Indeed, we may even have mixed emotions regarding the matter, because we may have reasons for wanting something to be true and yet also have other reasons for wanting it to be false. For example, Frank has been having a lot of health problems and so he consults his doctor. After running a series of tests, the doctor sends Frank to an oncologist, because she suspects that Frank may have a rare form of cancer. In one sense, Frank would like the matter to be closed, because he wants to find out what is wrong with him and proceed with the treatment. Nevertheless, the thought of having cancer upsets Frank greatly, and he hopes that his problem is less serious. Even though Frank does not know what is best and what to believe, he still understands that this is a serious matter, and so he cares about it deeply.

If an issue is important to us, then we will be emotionally invested in it regardless of the conclusions that we reach. Some issues, such as abortion, are thus very polarizing. People on both sides are rather adamant about their views, because they feel that a lot is at stake. This trend is related to a basic tenet of psychology: the opposite of love is not hate, but indifference. Hatred actually discloses deep feelings which have been thwarted in some way. This insight is used frequently in marital counselling situations. If a couple demonstrate feelings of resentment and hurt, then it indicates that they still care about the relationship, and this may give some hope of patching things up. However, if they are indifferent about their difficulties, they will most likely not be motivated to work towards restoring the relationship.

It has been said that opinions are like noses – everybody has one. As we have already noted, that is not quite true, because we might be undecided about certain matters. However, one thing is true in all cases. The positions that people take on a given issue do not indicate how important the issue is to them. We can be strongly supportive, opposed, or undecided. Likewise, we can be weakly supportive, opposed, or undecided. However, when we care more about an issue, we will be motivated to come to some kind of conclusion. For instance, people who feel that abortion is an important issue will be more motivated to form their own positions regarding it. The importance that beliefs have for us is evident not only in our desire to form conclusions, but also in our desire to defend these conclusions. It is consequently difficult for us not to become defensive about things that we care about very deeply.

REASONS FOR BELIEVING

There may be a number of reasons why we might adhere to a particular belief, so it would be futile to attempt to assemble a comprehensive list. Rather, I will simply discuss some of the more common reasons that we have for believing something. The ability to identify and scrutinize the reasons that we have for embracing certain beliefs is an important step towards intellectual maturity. Our beliefs are necessarily intertwined, and since our reasons for embracing these beliefs are actually simpler, more fundamental beliefs, our reasons are intertwined as well. This poses some difficulty in evaluating and improving our beliefs, but it by no means makes the task impossible.

We believe some things simply because *we are convinced that they are true*. We form a conclusion based on the available evidence, and then we live with it. This can give us either a positive or a negative feeling. There are some things that we gladly accept as true, but there are other things that we regretfully accept as true. Suppose a married woman suspects her husband of having an affair behind her back and hires a private investigator to find out what is going on. If she loves her husband, then she will be relieved if she discovers that his secretive behaviour is because he has been planning a surprise birthday party for her. On the other hand, she will be distraught if her suspicions are confirmed. If she wishes to be objective (something that must also be desired), she will accept the truth no matter what it is.

Of course, people often do not wish to be objective, and so their beliefs are held for other reasons. There are times when cherished beliefs start to falter, because we are less certain of them than we were previously and/or we are increasingly convinced that they are not true at all. In such cases, even though we might have a genuine regard for truth, it would not be uncommon to find the loss of certainty unsettling, to say the least, and we may continue to hold these beliefs simply because *we want them to be true*. Sometimes this is very subjective and self-serving. We choose to believe things not because we are truly convinced of their factuality, but because we consider it beneficial to do so. For one thing, many of our beliefs become *tied to our self-esteem*. For whatever reason, we feel better about ourselves when we espouse particular beliefs. This dynamic is rather obvious in persons who never admit that they might be wrong. For them, an admission of fallibility would be a blow to their self-esteem.

Another common example of this dynamic is *group identification*. The old saying 'Birds of a feather flock together' is largely true, because we do tend to associate with those who think like us. It makes it easier for us to interpret life's experiences and cope with the difficulties we encounter. Group identification is very beneficial, but only to a limited extent. On the one hand, it is very difficult to learn from and relate to people whose beliefs are vastly different from ours, so we need interaction with others who share at least some of our beliefs, especially the beliefs that are more foundational to our overall belief structure. On the other hand, relating to people who do not think like us allows our beliefs to be challenged, and this often forces us to reconsider some of the beliefs we hold. Moreover, our perspective broadens as we are able to understand the perspectives of others.

Consequently, group interaction can stimulate intellectual growth when there is an accepted basis for dialogue, but not uniform agreement. However, this benefit is lost altogether if group members are not truly interested in growing intellectually. In fact, it is often the case that although some group members may share the commitment to intellectual growth, it is by no means embraced by everyone. Individuals must often be willing to stand against the group (or, as Plato put it, 'the herd'). Regardless of whether the group dynamics are intellectually stimulating or stifling, intellectual progress requires individuals to think for themselves. Beliefs cannot be embraced simply because they are a part of group identity.

Another subjective reason for embracing beliefs is the fact that we often *associate beliefs with specific people*. Beliefs can be associated with parents, teachers, friends, clergy, physicians, etc. Whenever beliefs are cherished by people we love and/or respect, rejecting their beliefs can seem like a subtle form of rejecting them. However, since belief itself is the way we attach meaning to life's experiences, perhaps the most common subjective reason that we desire to believe certain things is that *beliefs function as a coping mechanism*, as I mentioned earlier. In fact, this motivation is so strong that we try to salvage our coping beliefs as long as possible, only abandoning them after they break down and cease to help us cope. This is why religious traditions which place greater demands upon their adherents characteristically generate conversions which are more dramatic. Since a much greater change is required, the motivation to change must be greater, and this usually begins with a major breakdown of previous coping mechanisms.

Atheists who disdain the faith of others fail to recognize this, or they are simply unsympathetic towards the way that religious belief helps many people cope with life. For those of us who live comfortable lives in comparison with many parts of the world, it seems rather egocentric and arrogant to trivialize the role of religious belief in lives that are not so comfortable or happy; it is their source of hope and inspiration. Moreover, religion often inspires us to strive to live by our highest ideals. Human beings have consistently demonstrated a desire to believe in something greater than themselves, and it is not apparent that this will die out any time soon. I am not convinced by the atheists who assume that religious belief itself will eventually become obsolete with sufficient intellectual progress. Rather, the non-empirical character of religious belief always allows room for some sense of awe and mystery, so long as one does not give up the struggle for truth and yield to a more comfortable scepticism or dogmatism.

Still, since our beliefs are all ultimately grounded in empirical experience, they are formed from our own perspectives. With only a few exceptions (e.g. mathematics, logic), all of our beliefs have some degree of subjectivity, so it is unreasonable to try to eliminate subjectivity altogether. Nevertheless, the interconnectedness of our beliefs makes subjectivity a real problem, because the subjectivity of one belief affects other beliefs as well. Consequently, ensuring the reliability of our beliefs requires us to monitor and limit their subjectivity. Every belief should have some objective basis, as much as possible. In consideration of its highly subjective nature, this is even more crucial in the realm of religious belief.

CHAPTER 2

MOVING BEYOND SIMPLISTIC BELIEFS

WHY PEOPLE HOLD ONTO SIMPLISTIC BELIEFS

As we have already noted, the desire to grow intellectually is by no means uniform or even widespread. As we shall see later, we are generally not afraid to embrace new beliefs as long as we can suitably incorporate them within the present belief structure. In other words, we are willing to accept new beliefs that tend to reinforce the beliefs that we already hold. Being confronted by new beliefs that challenge our present beliefs is a different story altogether, because it forces a number of beliefs to be reformulated. As a result, embracing new beliefs per se is not a problem in the vast majority of instances. The real obstacle to intellectual growth is our unwillingness to change our beliefs when they prove to be inadequate.

Many people are reluctant to relinquish their beliefs, some even to the extent of opposing intellectual progress altogether. On the one hand, this reluctance can be a general resistance to changing beliefs, and this can stem from a number of motives. In the first place, intellectual progress often gets stymied by *intellectual laziness*. The common motto of the intellectually lazy is 'If it's not broken, don't fix it.' They do not want to be bothered with reconsidering their beliefs, because this requires a lot of time and effort. As long as their beliefs function to their satisfaction, they are not motivated to scrutinize them in any meaningful way. This often leads to crisis management, because beliefs are only abandoned after they break down and fail to perform their function.

Closely related to intellectual laziness is the attitude of *irresponsibility*. Those who are guilty of this do not accept responsibility for their beliefs and/or their actions. They may be content to live with faulty or simplistic beliefs as long as their beliefs perform their desired function. However, the beliefs of each individual often affect other people, and this influence carries with it a corresponding level of responsibility. Parents, teachers and clergy are among those who bear greater intellectual responsibility, because they have more opportunity to affect the thinking of others. However, this is not the only type of intellectual irresponsibility. There are those who refuse to change their beliefs because they will not accept the responsibility of altering their behaviour to coincide with new beliefs. They would rather not be burdened.

Besides laziness and irresponsibility, there are two other basic emotions which can motivate us to resist changing our beliefs. First, *pride* becomes a factor when beliefs are tied to one's self-esteem. Under such circumstances, surrendering beliefs is seen as a threat to self-esteem. In order to protect self-esteem, the belief must also be protected and defended. Second, *fear* is also a strong motivator in resisting intellectual growth. Fear emerges when there is a perceived danger to personal well-being. In essence, relinquishing beliefs results in a loss of security, so every effort is made to preserve the beliefs for as long as possible.

The motivations of pride and fear surface in a number of ways and hence fuel several other attitudes. For one thing, some people are *reluctant to admit that they are wrong*. Indeed, there are those who are so adamant that they refuse to allow even the mere possibility of being mistaken. On the one hand, this could be a matter of pride. Somehow they believe that being wrong will decrease their self-worth. On the other hand, this type of perfectionism can also be rooted in fear. People who suffer from this attitude do not have a reliable, rational basis for their beliefs, so they must defend them out of sheer passion. Deep down they know that their beliefs cannot be supported, so they refuse to entertain the possibility of the beliefs being faulty. It is frequently the case that when some beliefs are defended without a rational basis, there are many other beliefs which also lack sufficient grounds of support. Calling any of the beliefs into question will ultimately threaten a number of other beliefs, maybe the entire belief structure.

Along similar lines, we are likely to become defensive and refuse to change our beliefs if we *lack the ability to understand more complex concepts*. Essentially, some people refuse to believe anything that they do not thoroughly understand, and this compels them to keep their beliefs sufficiently simple so that they can manage them. This is ultimately an *unwillingness to rely on others*, because we must trust others in matters that exceed our own understanding. Once again, this can be fuelled by pride or by fear. We might be too proud to be dependent upon the thinking of others, or we might be fearful of any such dependency. It seems that a limited amount of this reluctance is desirable. We should not be naive and simply believe everything that is presented to us. Nevertheless, it is foolish to be critical to the point of rejecting perfectly valid, trustworthy information.

The reluctance to relinquish beliefs can also be specific. We can be opposed to changing particular beliefs, especially if we do not see the benefit of the change. Quite often it is not apparent how changing beliefs can lead to a better state of affairs, and there is therefore insufficient motivation to make the change. This may help to explain why people tend to hold onto their beliefs for as long as possible, until the beliefs break down and must be abandoned. This reveals a tendency among many people to adhere to beliefs of which they have little or no certainty. As we have already noted, there is a difference between believing something because we are convinced that it is true and believing it merely because we want it to be true.

Let us return for a moment to the premise that belief is the foundation of our knowledge and our behaviour. Every belief is rooted in basic perceptions and is interrelated with our other beliefs. This is what enables us to make sense of life's experiences. As a result, belief is rudimentary to our motives as well, so when we speak of the reasons we have for believing certain things, we are in effect referring to prior beliefs that are more basic. Although human motivation is somewhat complex, it is sufficient for this discussion to observe that all motivation is grounded in some type of anticipated pleasure, whether it be concrete or abstract, narrow or broad.

Some thinkers contend that the only true motive is one's own well-being and happiness. They claim that there is no such thing as genuine altruism, since everything boils down to narrow self-interest. According to this theory, even martyrs sacrifice their lives because they derive some type of personal pleasure from their apparent heroism, perhaps the hope of eternal life, the satisfaction of being admired by others, etc. This theory is referred to as *psychological egoism*. The arguments advanced by psychological egoists are rather compelling. There does not seem to be such a thing as a purely *selfless* act, since all motivation is ultimately driven by some type of pleasure.

However, psychological egoism falls short in its analysis, because an act does not need to be *selfless* in order to be *unselfish*. The pleasure that is derived from it can simply be the satisfaction of benefiting someone else, promoting the common good, pleasing God, doing the ethical thing, etc. We can have values that transcend our personal interests, values that we consider to be more important than our own well-being and happiness. This enables us to make sacrifices and perform thankless tasks. Religious belief is often fuelled by this kind of motivation. Indeed, this is strongly advocated in the Sermon on the Mount.

Of course, we still cannot deny the pervasiveness of self-interest. Christian ethicist Reinhold Niebuhr drew attention to this. In fact, religious people in general often try to justify their actions and attitudes by claiming that they conform to God's will, but it is rather obvious to others that this is merely a way to legitimate what they really want to do deep down. For example, I once heard the following advice being given to a group of young adults: 'Make sure that you pray about the decision to get married, because God has someone picked out for you specifically, but don't worry, God won't pick someone for you that you find unattractive.' This essentially means that religious people really choose to marry people whom they find attractive, then they justify their decisions by convincing themselves that 'it is God's will'. It is astounding how many people climb social ladders, make strategic career moves, and live materialistic, hedonistic lifestyles while claiming that such is 'God's will' for them. It is quite convenient indeed, especially when it is inconsistent with the religious beliefs that they claim to embrace.

Among those that are aware of this tendency, some still adhere to the notion that God has some specific custom-made plan for their lives. Consequently, they struggle with every decision, trying to determine whether they are following God's will or their own. They realize the constant influence of our own self-interest, and they also realize our inability to objectively discern 'God's will' in a given situation (assuming that God has specific expectations in the first place). In the end, these people are left with a rather schizophrenic type of religious experience. If they can identify the pleasure that they are deriving from a particular decision, they will conclude that they are following their own will, not God's will.

They only have several ways for avoiding this dilemma. First, they can take the hard, ascetic path in life, one that they would not otherwise choose for themselves. This will assure them that they are not following their own will. However, they can only see this as God's will if they also believe that God wants them to take the rough road. Kierkegaard believed that God does expect this of everyone, but many find this conclusion unsettling. Instead, it is a common belief that God calls specific people (e.g. those called into full-time ministry) to lives of sacrifice. Those who feel too guilty to allow the sacrificial life of ministry to be left to others consequently discern this guilt as God's call on their lives. The rest are relieved that the responsibility is not theirs to bear. Second, this dilemma can be resolved by relinquishing the notion that God has a specific plan and set of expectations for each person. Instead, 'God's will' can be seen as more general, applying to humanity as a whole, not to specific individuals. This gives people the freedom to live their lives without this schizophrenic struggle. Third, the dilemma goes away when we conclude that it is actually 'God's will' for us to be happy. People can choose the path to pleasure and prosperity and see it all as God's blessings on their lives. I believe that this is how most people deal with the dilemma, because this is seemingly the reason why religion frequently functions as a justification for the hedonism that people are inclined to pursue anyway.

In the previous chapter, we identified a number of common reasons that people have for holding beliefs. Since these reasons are themselves beliefs, every one of them is likewise grounded in perceptions and beliefs that are more basic, and each one is based on some type of pleasure. Some beliefs are embraced because they are genuinely regarded as being true. Here the basic motivation is a desire to conform to truth. Even this desire can be narrowly self-interested, because people can and actually should consider it in their best interests to live in accordance with truth. However, truth itself is a higher ideal and is thus a universal concept (even though people may disagree as to what can be regarded as true). This is why we generally consider a desire for truth to be more objective than subjective.

All of this analysis boils down to a simple fact. On the one hand, we may hold specific beliefs for reasons that are more objective, and this essentially stems from a desire to respect values that we recognize as being greater than our own narrow interests. On the other hand, beliefs may be held for selfish reasons, even if the reasons themselves generally tend towards objectivity and universality. Let us consider a common example. Susan believes that the Bible is divinely inspired, and she is genuinely convinced of this. As such, she regards the Bible as authoritative both for her personally and for humanity in general. For her the Bible provides an objective reference that guides her in her daily life, informing her ethics and lifestyle. Moreover, due to the fact that she regards the Bible as inspired by God, she believes that it reveals ultimate truth and reality. Even though Susan's beliefs do indeed tend towards objectivity and universality, she may still have selfish reasons for believing in the authority of the Bible. This belief may be a central part of her family heritage and foundational to her religious beliefs in general. She may also embrace the Bible simply because it helps her to cope with her problems, gives her hope in every situation, and brings peace, contentment and meaning in her daily life. These subjective reasons for believing are certainly worthwhile in their own right, but belief itself becomes merely subjective when it is predominantly motivated by narrowly self-interested reasons. Without a doubt, a number of Christians will object to my analysis. Nevertheless, would they not applaud it if the example focused not on the Bible but on the Qur'an or the Book of Mormon?

As a general rule, the more we perceive that particular beliefs are related to our well-being and happiness, the more tenaciously we guard and defend them. This is certainly true with respect to the reasons for believing that were discussed in the previous chapter, and it is likewise true for many other reasons that we have for believing. Given the fact that our subjective reasons for believing are all tied to perceptions of our own well-being and happiness, we can expect this subjectivity to be identifiable by the emotions that arise when these beliefs are either supported or threatened. Whenever we perceive that our well-being and happiness are being promoted, positive emotions will result, all expressing some form of *happiness* (e.g. *joy, tranquility, congeniality, gratitude, hope*). In contrast, when we believe that our well-being or happiness is under attack, this perception will produce negative emotions. *Fear* and *anger* are two of the more common negative emotions, but we might also expect to see specific forms of them, such as *depression, uncertainty, worry* and *hatred*.

Some argue that the subjective element of belief ensures that we all have some disconnection between what we claim and what we truly believe deep down within us. In other words, the claim is that since we have both objective and subjective reasons for believing in general, we end up having two sets of beliefs, one that we regard as objectively true and one that we merely wish were true. To be sure, this can and does indeed happen all too often. People who hold beliefs primarily on subjective grounds avoid discussing their beliefs on objective grounds, because deep down they realize that their beliefs lack an objective basis.

In addition to this type of breach in the belief structure, there are also gaps that naturally occur as the result of doubt. We are not omniscient, and we cannot know things infallibly. We are all susceptible to mistakes and errors. Consequently, there is some room for even the slightest degree of doubt in our most reliable beliefs, those of which we are most certain. For many of our beliefs, the room for doubt is greater still. We routinely live with a certain amount of doubt. All belief requires some level of trust and involves a degree of risk. Pragmatists like Peirce, James and Dewey were effective in pointing this out. According to James, evidence can only compel us to believe up to a certain point. Very few things (e.g. mathematical and logical laws) can be proved rationally to the level of absolute certainty. (A few sceptical theorists even question this.) Believing thus requires an act of the will, an exercise of trust.

Nevertheless, pragmatists like James did not sufficiently recognize the proper limits of subjectivity. Once the doubt we have regarding a certain belief becomes great enough, accepting that belief by a sheer act of will (i.e. on predominantly subjective grounds) will cause the same kind of rift in the belief structure. There will indeed be a disconnection between beliefs that we are convinced are true and beliefs that we want to be true in spite of the absence of this kind of conviction. This does not need to be the case. Intellectual honesty can help to bridge these gaps and build integrity within the entire belief structure. In the final analysis, there is a subjective element in all of our beliefs, due to our epistemic limits. This allows small gaps to exist in the belief structure, and these gaps cannot be eliminated altogether, only minimized. The problem is only intensified when we stop striving for objectivity in our beliefs, choosing rather to believe on subjective grounds.

REASONS FOR EMBRACING NEW CONCEPTS

Seeing the benefits of changing our beliefs motivates us to leave old beliefs behind and accept new beliefs in their place. The problem is that many people do not really see the benefits of changing their beliefs, so they insist on adapting and retaining their present beliefs for as long as possible. Obviously, I cannot talk about specific reasons that people might have for accepting particular beliefs, but I would like to briefly mention a few benefits of embracing new beliefs in general. These points will be more or less relevant for individual beliefs, depending upon the circumstances, so this is not intended to be a set of criteria which should strictly be applied to particular instances. However, in addressing the general benefits of embracing new beliefs, a case will be made for intellectual progress. Even when we may not see the need to change particular beliefs that we hold, we should still desire to progress intellectually and be willing to reconsider our beliefs if there is sufficient reason to do so.

As we have just observed, each belief structure naturally has gaps in it, and the greater these gaps are, either in size or in number, the less stable the overall structure will be. Consequently, reducing these gaps can *enhance the stability of the belief structure*, and the way that this is generally accomplished is through the incorporation of new beliefs. Since all beliefs are synthesized from other simpler beliefs, new beliefs that replace older beliefs by and large are more complex than the beliefs they replace. They take new information into account that older beliefs cannot adequately explain or assimilate. As a result, new beliefs enable us to reduce the gaps that exist in the overall belief structure, and this helps to stabilize it.

We never do reach a point of infallibility in our beliefs, so we never achieve absolute certainty or stability. In fact, the stability of the belief structure is never permanent but is constantly changing, because everything around us is in a constant state of change, and we are continuously confronted with new information that we must process. The stability of the belief structure is always being challenged, so the goal is not to reach some level of certainty at which we can cast off responsibility for our beliefs and become intellectually lazy. Instead, we should seek to increase the stability of the belief structure by deepening and broadening it. It can be deepened as we improve the reasons we have for embracing particular beliefs, and it can be broadened as we expand our perspective and take a wider array of information into account.

Increasing the stability of the belief structure not only gives greater intellectual stability, but it *helps to stabilize the emotions* as well. Our well-being and happiness are not as vulnerable when our beliefs are more stable. As we refine and stabilize our beliefs over time, the less drastically they need to be changed. In other words, although mature beliefs may still be altered as often as (or even more often than) immature beliefs, the alterations themselves become smaller. Unrefined beliefs are subject to major revisions, and they are much more likely to be rejected altogether. If we revise our beliefs conscientiously, taking into account all the information we have at a given point in time, it becomes more likely that future revisions will be lesser in degree. Since a refined belief is one that has already been scrutinized and adjusted a number of times, it is less likely to require a major revision. In fact, the revisions become smaller and smaller, even though they may occur more frequently.

Embracing new beliefs also *increases the comprehensiveness of the belief structure*. This follows from what has just been said. As our beliefs integrate more information, our intellectual perspective is consequently broadened. We are not only enabled to make sense of more things we experience, but we are also better equipped to relate our beliefs to new experiences. In effect, the belief structure becomes more versatile and flexible, and this in turn adds to the strength and stability of the overall structure.

All of these reasons for adopting new beliefs have something in common. They all help to illustrate how intellectual progress *brings inner freedom to the individual*. The truth does indeed set us free. It helps to release us from fear and vulnerability, from control and dependence, and from false expectations and hopes. Embracing the truth can be very sobering, but it is also very liberating. In the absence of intellectual maturity, we construct a false reality bedecked with artificial expectations, and this is a laborious process. However, embracing truth in epistemic humility can deliver us from such demands and instability.

EXCEPTIONS

Adopting new beliefs does not always produce these effects. There are several situations in which this is true. First, *formulating first-time beliefs* does not usually foster intellectual maturity, because first-time beliefs themselves are unrefined. However, the development of brand new beliefs is a mark of intellectual progress, for they serve as signposts of travels into unfamiliar territory. Although first-time beliefs tend initially to lessen the stability of the belief structure, they further its long-term stability after they have been refined and developed. As we mature intellectually, even the quality of our first-time beliefs should improve, because the process of forming beliefs will be more mature. Mature thinkers can thus refine brand new beliefs more quickly and easily than immature thinkers.

Second, intellectual maturity is not enhanced whenever *beliefs are formulated or replaced without due scrutiny*. Simply having new beliefs does not represent an improved state of affairs. Rather, the belief structure is improved when the beliefs within it are stronger individually and as a cohesive whole. Beliefs must be refined and revised, and this requires scrutiny and critical thinking. As the old saying goes, 'No pain, no gain'. It is certainly easier to accept beliefs uncritically, but this does nothing to substantively improve the quality of either the beliefs themselves or the structure overall.

Third, the process of *discovering and correcting a bad belief structure* naturally leads to greater instability up front, even though the eventual pay-off will be quite the opposite. As we mature intellectually, we must evaluate the beliefs that we have been taught since childhood. Whenever we conclude that the beliefs that we have been given are faulty or incorrect, a commitment to intellectual maturity requires us to correct beliefs that are faulty and abandon those which are altogether incorrect or otherwise insufficient. In the early stages of this process, we may have more inadequate beliefs than we do beliefs that are reliable. However, a turning point is eventually reached when the majority of our beliefs are reliable. Before this turning point, progress entails increased doubt and uncertainty, but after the turning point, the process is reversed, and stability and certainty start to be increased.

THE DIFFICULTY OF REPLACING RELIGIOUS BELIEFS

In all fairness, the reluctance to alter and replace faulty religious beliefs is understandable, because the task has inherent difficulties. The *nature of religious belief* in particular makes the process of intellectual maturity more complicated. We cherish our religious beliefs more dearly than most of our other beliefs, since religion focuses on that which we regard as *sacred and ultimately meaningful*. Moreover, as I indicated earlier, religion serves several important psychological functions. Among other things, it provides us with: 1) a sense of identity and self-image; 2) a frame of reference for determining the meaning of life and its experiences; 3) a mechanism for coping with life's problems, and especially a sense of hope; and 4) a means of either unifying us with or separating us from other people. As a result, we more quickly accept and more slowly reject religious tenets that more effectively perform these functions for us personally. Inversely, we are slow to accept and quick to reject religious tenets that hinder these functions for us personally.

Here is a simple example. One of Linda's children is diagnosed with terminal cancer. Her faith in supernatural divine healing gives her a sense of hope, allowing her to maintain a positive outlook and not to be overcome with grief or depression. Linda does everything that she can to meet the conditions that are a part of her belief (prayer, faith, etc.), but the child eventually dies. Now she must cope with the death itself as a present reality (and no longer an anticipated one), and a number of religious beliefs might help her to do this. For instance, she might consider the child's death to be a blessing in disguise, regarding the child as better off in some way. After all, an eternity in heaven far outweighs anything that this life can offer. Moreover, perhaps the child was delivered from a worse fate. Linda might also regard the death in a fatalistic way as a part of God's will and simply refuse to make any further sense of it. However, Linda could also blame her belief in divine healing for adding to her grief, and this could lead her to abandon it.

Suppose now that one year later another of Linda's children is diagnosed with the same type of terminal cancer. It is very unlikely that Linda's religious beliefs regarding this matter will be unchanged from the previous instance. She has probably adapted them in some way in an attempt to find a better way to cope with the new circumstance. On the one hand, if she values the sense of hope and positive outlook that the previous belief provided, she will not want to abandon it. On the other hand, if she wishes to avoid the pain of unfulfilled expectations, then she will minimize or eliminate her belief in supernatural divine healing. Nevertheless, it is very likely that she will retain a moderated version of the previous belief, maintaining but limiting the expectation of supernatural intervention.

This brief analysis still only gives a partial picture of Linda's motivations. Since her belief in divine healing is a part of her broader view of divine providence, it ultimately reflects something about the nature of God. Consequently, the belief in divine healing has a sacred element, i.e. the nature of God, and Linda may be reluctant to question the conception of God that she has learned from her parents, from her church, or from others that she loves and respects. Even if she is willing to change this conception, it is a change that she will not take lightly, due to its sacredness.

In other words, the more important our beliefs are to us, the more protective of them we will be. Religion is not studied critically in many traditions for that reason. In fact, religious traditions that more heavily emphasize religious education for their children and youth are quite often the most resistant to change. They may be open to change in many areas of knowledge, but the realm of religious belief is most sacrosanct and cannot be violated, and since religious belief is largely a matter of faith, it is regarded as blasphemous even to question religious teachings, because that would signify at the very least a lack of faith.

Religious belief is also difficult to refine due to its *metaphysical character*. It deals with realities and concepts which are beyond the realm of our sensory perception. In essence, it cannot be determined empirically. With regard to beliefs such as the existence of God, the reality of an afterlife, and the actuality of supernatural intervention, none of these can be proved or disproved on empirical grounds. They are matters of faith. The same holds true for our religious beliefs in general. We can neither prove nor disprove them, and so they are by nature *highly speculative* in comparison with most other types of belief. This brings us back to the premise that religious belief is rather subjective. Many embrace this and regard religious truth as merely relative. Those who reject this conclusion must establish some kind of objectivity in their religious beliefs. One option is to rest on *foundationalism*, uncritically accepting certain sources as wholly trustworthy, perhaps even infallible or inerrant. Examples of these sources include Scripture, tradition, orthodoxy and the Church. Later I will suggest that foundations are necessary, but it is intellectually immature to accept a source uncritically.

Another difficulty with replacing our religious beliefs stems from their *interconnectedness*. Challenging one belief inevitably leads to challenging other beliefs. Sometimes even the foundations are questioned. The greater the number of beliefs that must be changed, the greater the impact will be on the belief structure as a whole. This impact will also be greater if key beliefs are called into question. All of this greatly complicates the process and becomes a strong disincentive against intellectual progress. A good example that illustrates this characteristic is the Roman Catholic ban on contraception. Catholic doctrine has traditionally taught that since the most integral part of sexual intercourse is procreation, sexual activity is only legitimate whenever there is a willingness to procreate, and this in turn is only legitimate within the confines of marriage. Only married couples can have sex, and they can only control the possibility of conception using natural means. The interesting thing is that the church's magisterium cannot lift the ban on contraception without opening the debate as to the legitimacy of sex apart from procreation, and if this were to be reconsidered, a number of other issues would also need to be revisited (e.g. homosexuality, masturbation).

Finally, beliefs are not likely to be changed unless we accept the *responsibility to adapt to new beliefs*. Sometimes we might not want to face up to the truth (as we understand it). In these situations, the temptation is to frantically avoid changing our beliefs, because this would either necessitate making changes in our lives that we do not want to make or else lead to a serious breach in the belief structure, causing a great rift between what we *want to believe* and what we *truly believe deep down*. It seems that some people are able to convince themselves that the change is unnecessary, and they continue to live in a perceived reality that increasingly becomes a product of their own imagination. In contrast, others find themselves unable to control their beliefs in this way; once they are exposed to new evidence, they cannot help but be compelled by it. Their beliefs change even though they may not want them to change. I really do not know how to explain the differences between these two dispositions, but it appears that the issue centres on which a person values more – belief or truth.

A familiar example

Jim is a college student majoring in physics at a public university. His religious background is Christian fundamentalism, and a crucial part of that heritage is a belief in the inerrancy of Scripture. Since he regards the Bible as verbally inspired by God, he has always interpreted the text literally. In fact, he was taught that affirming anything less about Scripture essentially questions its authority altogether. In the course of his studies Jim is confronted with the theory of evolution. It would be easy for him to deal with the subject were he to find the evidence in support of evolution unconvincing. However, Jim finds the case for evolution to be rather compelling from a scientific perspective.

If Jim does not attempt to resolve his conflicting beliefs, there will be a serious gap in his belief structure. His options for this resolution basically fit into one of the following categories: 1) show that the beliefs are really compatible; 2) reject one belief in order to fully embrace the other; or 3) modify at least one of the beliefs in order to reconcile them. Given his literalist view of Scripture, the first option does not seem possible. Ironically, early fundamentalists like Benjamin Warfield were open to the possibility of evolution if it resulted in a literal Adam and Eve as the first evolved human pair. A century later, this does not seem scientifically feasible, in Jim's opinion, and so he is left with the latter two options.

Suppose Jim chooses one belief at the expense of the other. He could completely give up his belief in the authority of Scripture and regard the creation narratives in the book of Genesis (1.1–2.3; 2.4–25) as mere myths, or he could find some reason to dismiss evolution from further consideration. If Jim wants his belief to be grounded in truth, he will need to give the various positions due consideration and weigh them in the most objective manner possible. The first thing that Jim notices is that the objections to evolution overwhelmingly (if not exclusively) come from fundamentalist Christians. They reject evolution for a number of reasons, but most of these are not scientific reasons. There are those (e.g. the Creation Science advocates) who interpret the data in a very different way from the scientific community at large, so Jim must take their explanations into consideration.

Beyond this, Jim finds that most of the reasons that people have for rejecting evolution do not address the theory's scientific basis. Rather, they either aim at discrediting science and scientists in general or they assert that historic Christian beliefs are somehow inerrant, at least in crucial doctrinal matters. Jim encounters claims like the following: 1) 'Evolutionists cannot be trusted, because they are all atheists'; 2) 'Scientific theories are always being revised, and since evolution is a relatively recent theory, it will eventually be overturned'; 3) 'Evolution cannot be true due to the fact that it contradicts several core doctrines of Christianity'; and 4) 'Christians have traditionally regarded the creation narratives as literal, historical events, and since the Church is guided by the Holy Spirit, Christian orthodoxy will eventually be proved once again to be correct'.

At the end of the day, Jim must decide whether he wants his beliefs to conform to truth, or his perception of truth to be determined by the beliefs he wishes to hold. If he chooses to pursue truth, he is indeed faced with the colossal task of sifting through these various assertions. In fact, the task is so daunting that it is not practical for him to tackle it on his own. After all, he is not a biologist, geologist, theologian, biblical scholar or Church historian. He realizes that the best thing that he can do is to make an informed decision based in part upon the expertise of others. Unfortunately, this is not an important part of his religious tradition, and most of his fellow believers prefer a simplistic, uncritical faith. They do not see the need for intellectual growth and development, and they refuse to face challenges in their own faith. Consequently, they are unable to help Jim to resolve his beliefs, and they are critical of his efforts to explore and question his own beliefs.

If Jim gives up on the quest for truth, it is highly probable that he (like others in his tradition) will start to retain his religious beliefs on subjective grounds. However, if he accepts the challenge, he will first learn that evolutionists are not all atheists. There are some atheists among them, but there are also many theistic evolutionists. Next, Jim will come to understand the processes by which scientific theories are formed and tested, and he can assess the strengths and weaknesses of the theory of evolution without making gross over-generalizations. Also, Jim can start to see through circular arguments such as 'The Bible is inspired by God because it says so in 2 Timothy 3.16' and 'We know that the Holy Spirit keeps the Church from error, because that is what Christians have always believed.'

Moreover, Jim will discover that many Christians over the years, including some notable figures in early Christian history, have interpreted the creation narratives symbolically. He will find out that many Christian thinkers have considered theological themes from an evolutionary perspective, even well before the time of Darwin. He will realize that Christians have consistently disagreed more than they have agreed. People have been castigated and even martyred for being heretics, including scientists like Galileo, who was condemned simply because he claimed that the earth is not at the centre of the universe. Should Jim decide to investigate the theological implications of evolution, he will see that it does indeed go well beyond the issue of interpreting biblical texts; a number of key doctrines are affected. However, he observes that non-fundamentalist Christian traditions have predominantly been wrestling with these issues for at least a century. Jim feels a sense of betrayal regarding his own tradition, because it cannot help him in his pursuit of the truth, at least in this matter.

When all is said and done, Jim chooses the last option, modifying his beliefs so that they will be compatible. He will find a way for Scripture and science to be in dialogue with one another, so that he will have a more holistic view of the truth. This will not be possible if he retreats to foundationalism, accepting either science or Scripture uncritically and allowing it to trump the other without qualification. The pursuit of truth must always be open-ended to some extent. Those who close themselves to the pursuit of truth either deny its possibility entirely, do not value it properly, or feel that they already know it and do not need to question their own beliefs. Hopefully, Jim will avoid these pitfalls and come to experience the freedom of living and growing in the pursuit of truth. However, if Jim decides not to resolve his conflict, choosing instead to leave his religious beliefs unaltered, he will be forced either to abandon them altogether or to defend them dogmatically on subjective grounds. The people in his tradition who do the latter will most likely be critical of him if he responds in any other way.

SECTION TWO

BELIEF IN HISTORICAL PERSPECTIVE

CHAPTER 3

RELIGIOUS BELIEF BEFORE THE ENLIGHTENMENT

Thus far we have discussed the nature of religious belief in general, noting the dynamics which hinder people in maturing intellectually. When we examine the process of maturing in our beliefs, it will be useful to do so from the perspective of the historical development of religious belief. This will help us to sort out the various types of religious belief that we encounter today, because they all have historical roots and precedents. Additionally, the way that people react to the intellectual climate of their own time says something about their own levels of maturity. As a general rule, humanity does continue to progress and develop over time, but this usually occurs over long periods of time, after intellectual movements stimulate an array of responses and subsequent counter-responses.

One of the most prominent intellectual trends today is postmodernism, regarded by many as the end of modernism. I am not convinced that this will be the long-term effect. Instead, I believe that postmodernism will serve as a strong corrective to the excessive optimism of modernism, and a more critical form of modernism will survive. However, it is not the goal of this book to resolve or fully address this or any of the other current debates on epistemology. This book is written to promote the intellectual maturity of the individual. My approach in matters of belief and knowledge (i.e. epistemology) is indeed more characteristic of modernism than it is of postmodernism, and I simply wish to be forthright with the reader in this regard.

Although I want to encourage my readers to engage in individual, critical thought, it is not my intention to champion any view in particular (regarding Scripture, tradition, spirituality, etc.). I feel that as we become more historically informed, our perspectives broaden, and this enables us to have opinions that are more refined and mature. This will not eliminate disagreements, because the uncertainty and subjectivity of belief always allow for this possibility, even when we try our best to be careful and objective. However, as our beliefs mature, we are better able to appreciate the perspectives of others, and this permits more meaningful dialogue to take place.

The next four chapters will thus be a short exposition of intellectual history as it has impacted religious belief. As I indicated in my Introduction, I am approaching this subject from the perspective of Christianity, so the historical religious background referenced will likewise be addressed from this perspective. In the interest of brevity, the discussion will be limited to general currents and trends. Although some issues might be a bit oversimplified, it is hoped that the reader will indulge me in my efforts to stay focused on more salient points. This will prevent me from spending the extra time that would be needed to give further detail and nuance to the material. However, every effort will be made to be accurate and fair in characterizing various thinkers and intellectual currents.

THE ANCIENT MINDSET

The religious beliefs of ancient cultures were passed down from generation to generation and were a significant part of these cultures as a whole. It is true of every culture that what cannot be understood through scientific inquiry must be either regarded as a mystery or explained by means of speculation and imagination. Consequently, the religious beliefs of ancient cultures had a strong tendency towards superstition. Since they lacked a direct empirical basis, these myths and legends could not be verified. However, they did have some basis in empirical observation; otherwise, they would not have any explanatory power. For instance, if an ancient culture believed that rainfall was caused by one of the gods crying, this would be based upon observations that: 1) crying produces tears; and 2) tears are a form of moisture similar to rain. A belief such as this would lead to the conclusion that rainfall indicates that the gods are displeased. Similar beliefs were likewise often formed about lightning, thunder, earthquakes and other natural phenomena. Beliefs like these were speculative not only with regard to the events that they sought to interpret, but also in asserting the existence of gods with personalities very similar to human beings.

We are by and large curious creatures that wish to understand, and perhaps two of the most difficult questions to answer in any situation are 'How?' and 'Why?' Religious belief helps us to answer these questions. In their attempt to understand *how* and *why* certain events took place, ancient people appealed to superstition, because they lacked the empirical means of deriving more reliable answers. Their inability to account for facts that they observed also limited them in controlling their circumstances and environment. Much of their lives lay beyond their control. Consequently, they typically embraced some form of fatalism, ascribing the cause of events to the gods or to nature itself. In fact, many ancient cultures mixed the two, regarding the gods as subject to natural laws and considering nature to be divine in some way (e.g. the ancient Egyptian belief that the Nile River is divine). The feeling of vulnerability that often accompanied such fatalism also added to the anxiety that ancient cultures felt in the presence of foreigners. Cultures that espoused opposing beliefs and practices were seen as a threat, and security sometimes entailed eliminating these threats in one way or another. They frequently believed that their military conquests indicated the superiority of their gods.

The ancient religious mindset also included a notion of justice, i.e. the victory of good over evil. Even in polytheistic systems, there was much hope that good deities would defeat evil deities. Human beings would be accountable for their moral conduct as well, being duly recompensed in the afterlife, through reincarnation, etc. The gods would communicate their will to human beings through select individuals. As cultures developed and became organized politically, it was not uncommon to regard monarchs as the mouthpieces of the gods. Indeed, the king's word was law, because it reflected the will of the gods. Sometimes other individuals were regarded as prophets. They spoke on behalf of the gods, keeping both the monarchs and the people accountable to the divine will. In the Old Testament, this pattern also included the role of priest. The prophet, priest and king were thus all intermediaries between God and the people, but they represented a separation of powers so as to provide greater accountability. Similar dynamics existed in other ancient religions.

Plato and Aristotle

An important philosophical development in the ancient world was the thought of Plato and Aristotle, which occurred about 400 years before the time of Christ. Even though volumes could be written about their influence on Western religious thought, two particular differences between them are especially pertinent to the general discussion. Plato claimed that there is a division between the eternal/spiritual and material realms, and that everything that we experience (in the material realm) is an imperfect reflection of some eternal reality. He also believed that all learning is a type of recollection, that knowledge is something that we possessed in our eternal selves before we became human beings and had our spirits imprisoned in bodies.

Aristotle (who was Plato's pupil) built on this philosophy, but he regarded all knowledge as empirical (i.e. rooted in sensory experience). This sharp distinction between Plato's and Aristotle's thought arguably fostered the development of two views of knowledge – rationalism and empiricism. Simply put, rationalists believe that we can understand things that we do not experience personally, but empiricists claim that all of our concepts are constructed in some way from basic sense perceptions that we attain throughout the course of our lives. Rationalists presume that we can logically prove some metaphysical assertions (e.g. the existence of God) based on an analysis of the concepts themselves, but empiricists largely regard this as nothing more than conjecture.

The other difference between Platonism and Aristotelianism that is worth mentioning here is the relative optimism and pessimism of each side. Platonism was frequently employed to reinforce a more intuitive (even mystical) view of knowledge. For the Platonist, learning is both active and passive, because some things cannot be pursued but must simply be experienced on a higher plane. For the Aristotelian, knowledge is more reflective than intuitive. Aristotle did conclude that the basic foundations of knowledge must be intuited, but the pursuit of knowledge is more active. This basic contrast between active and passive views of knowledge can be seen in aesthetics. Some believe that beauty cannot be analysed, but must simply be experienced. For them, beauty is in the whole itself, not in the sum of its parts. In contrast, others believe that the more we understand a work of art or music, the better we can appreciate it. They claim that simple experience is shallow and self-centered. A similar division exists in views of spirituality. Do we simply experience God, or do we come to know God incrementally? Is attaining knowledge of God more passive or active?

THE MEDIEVAL PERIOD

In its early history, Christianity survived and flourished at the cost of much bloodshed as Christians were martyred for their faith within the Roman Empire. The early Christians proclaimed their faith at great personal risk and sacrifice. However, Christianity as a whole was rather fragmented, evidenced by the numerous factions that were separated over doctrinal disputes. All of this changed drastically in the early fourth century with the reign of Constantine, who gave Christianity protected status with the government. Councils were held to resolve the doctrinal disputes that had tended to divide Christians. Christianity became highly institutionalized, eventually merging Church and state in the Holy Roman Empire.

The most significant Christian thinker during this time period was Augustine (354–430), and his influence facilitated the elevation of the role of the Church and the decline of the role of the individual. The medieval Church was very hierarchical, teaching that authority is given by God to the Church, not to individuals. Christ authorized the apostles, they authorized their successors, and so forth. This is the doctrine of apostolic succession, which claims that Catholic priests alone are the true successors to the apostles, thus being the only ones authorized to administer the sacraments. Moreover, God speaks to individuals through the Church, which is both mother and teacher. The laity can trust the instruction of the Church, because the Church itself is holy and infallible. (This teaching culminated in the doctrine of papal infallibility.)

In the ancient world, it was believed that the gods speak through specially chosen individuals. Philosophy such as that advanced by thinkers like Plato and Aristotle counteracted this by creating some impetus for the development of individual thought and democracy, but this was quickly squelched under the iron wheel of the Roman Empire. The early Christians had come under the influence of Hellenism and tended to be rather free-thinking, but this splintered Christianity as a whole. The state Church of the medieval period brought unity, but it did so at the expense of free thought on the part of individuals. The doctrine of the infallibility of the Church was thus a reversion back to an earlier mindset.

This high view of Church authority was counterbalanced with Augustine's pessimistic view of human nature. He felt that human beings are completely depraved, perpetually inclined to sin, so much so that even our reasoning itself is tainted. Individual thought cannot be trusted. Rather, the individual's responsibility is to submit to the authority of the holy, infallible Church. The medieval period was thus a time when lay people were not trusted to read and inter-pret Scripture for themselves. The text was preserved from Jerome's *Vulgate*, which was a translation in Latin, a language accessible to only the educated clerics.

The medieval Church also gave rise to the Inquisition. Dissenters were condemned and sometimes executed for heresy. Scientists who contradicted the Church's official teachings were eschewed, includ-ing Galileo, who was excommunicated just for asserting that the earth revolves around the sun, not vice versa. Rather than pursue truth, the Church chose to defend belief. In reality, the Church was defending its own claims of authority and infallibility. Instead of developing beliefs that have a stronger empirical basis, the Church opted for beliefs that rested more on speculation.

This trend likewise reinforced the increase of mysticism during this period, both within the rituals of the Church and within the spirituality that was advocated in some of the monasteries. Various practices were regarded as invoking supernatural activity. The greater the emphasis given to the supernatural, the less emphasis the natural received. A clear example of such mysticism is the Catholic doctrine of transubstantiation (the claim that the bread and wine of Eucharist become the body and blood of Christ). At times mysti-cism is so imaginative that it is nothing more than mere superstition, as it is in practices such as burying a statue of St Joseph in the back yard of a house that one is trying to sell. (Of course, this is merely a private custom, not officially encouraged or advocated in any way.)

SCHOLASTICISM

Scholasticism arguably began with the rediscovery of the writings of Aristotle in the late medieval period. Muslims had already had access to them for some time, and they made several notable innov-ations (e.g. the development of algebra) before their Western coun-terparts. In time Jewish and Christian scholars were able to translate Aristotle's philosophy into Latin, and this opened new doors of aca-demic possibility. The Christians especially began to found universi-ties and to integrate theology with other disciplines of knowledge, including philosophy (which still included natural science at that point in time). Christian scholars started to believe that truth can be discovered in many ways and is not restricted to special revelation expressed through sacred texts. This was a stark contrast to Christianity in its prior neo-Platonic framework, in which knowledge is bifurcated into two realms: God's perfect truth and humanity's imperfect, sinful thinking.

The scholastic period was thus characterized by a greater trust in reason. Human beings were still regarded as sinful, but no longer seen as utterly depraved. According to the more pessimistic view, human reason is so corrupt that it cannot have any knowledge of God without special revelation (i.e. God revealed in Christ and in Scripture). As a more favourable model of human nature emerged, a place was given for natural revelation. In other words, God is revealed in creation, and human reason is thus able to comprehend God to a great extent through nature. The development of this line of thought became the foundation for natural law ethics, the teaching that right and wrong can be discerned in nature itself. In this new, more optimistic conception of humanity, every person is likewise naturally capable of some degree of morality. This is a clear departure from the more negative view, which contends that human beings cannot be virtuous without some supernatural dispensation of grace.

The scholastic thinkers consequently saw a benefit in integrating theology with other disciplines of knowledge, especially philosophy. For instance, Aquinas (1225?–74) effectively synthesized the thought of Augustine (and other Church Fathers) with the philosophy of Aristotle. Consequently, his writings did not receive widespread acclaim at first. Many felt that he had corrupted theology by mixing it with 'pagan' thought. Fortunately, Aquinas's theology eventually became the standard for Catholicism and has been a formidable influence on Christian thought in general.

During this period, many thinkers were dedicated to systematizing theology in a comprehensive manner. They are sometimes referred to as 'encyclopedists' because they tried to cover theology from 'A' to 'Z'. In many ways, scholasticism produced a solid foundation for future intellectual developments. Nevertheless, the thought of this period typically had two shortcomings. First, in their attempt to approach theology comprehensively, the scholastics frequently spent too much time focusing on the trivial. In their writings we find them contemplating questions such as 'How many angels can sit on the head of a pin?' and 'In the final resurrection, will we regain our hair and fingernail clippings?' Second, a number of scholastic thinkers wrote in service to the Church. To that extent they tended to function as apologists, not as constructive thinkers. They concocted some rather complex polemics at many points. For example, Aquinas went to great lengths in his attempt to demonstrate how the Eucharist can have the *form* of bread and wine but still have the *substance* of the body and blood of Christ. In other words, his explanation was necessarily convoluted, since he was trying to prove something that is otherwise counter-intuitive. In spite of all this wasted intellectual energy, however, the scholastic period was a still a huge step in the direction of free thought.

THE RENAISSANCE

The Renaissance continued and heightened the emphasis on human potential and goodness, culminating in the emergence of *humanism*. It was a time of scientific discovery, artistic expression, and exploration. There was a renewed interest in classical studies, especially the art, literature and civilization of ancient Greece and Rome. Faith in human knowledge and achievements only grew as scientists developed new theories, artists and musicians broadened aesthetic experience, and travellers colonized new lands. Much of Renaissance humanism tended to separate the sacred from the secular, and this helped to polarize the Church-state, which was beginning to lose its grip of control. Many people regarded this as a positive development, because they believed that the Church and its teachings were overreaching and needed to be curbed. Others saw the Renaissance as a threat to the sacred, undercutting the authority of the Church and theology.

THE REFORMATION

The Protestant Reformation, which began in 1517, is truly a most interesting development with respect to the unfolding of intellectual history. In some ways it continued the impetus of the Renaissance. To start, it tolled the death knell of the Holy Roman Empire, which had already started to disintegrate. Essentially, the high medieval view of authority was rejected. There was no longer a tacit acceptance of the Church or clergy as necessary intermediaries between God and the individual. Each person was now believed to be directly accountable to God. This helped to fuel the growing movement towards democratization. More specifically, it set the stage for the advancement of free thought, not only affecting the educated classes, but also giving the less educated more confidence in asserting their own opinions, particularly in matters of religion.

Nonetheless, the Reformation was in part a reaction against Renaissance humanism. It reverted back to medieval thought, especially the thought of Augustine, in several ways. For example, the Reformers once again stressed the total depravity of the individual. Moreover, they predominantly embraced predestinationism, a form of fatalism. This ran counter to the increasingly naturalistic world-view that was the result of scientific and technological advancement. In fact, the polarization between mysticism and naturalism increased during this period. Some people saw less of a need to attribute events to supernatural activity, but others preferred to regard daily events as a part of the all-encompassing divine will.

Overall, the Reformation rejected Renaissance humanism and reverted to the medieval mindset, and yet it simultaneously rejected the foundations which had supported the medieval thought to which it appealed. In the medieval period, teachings were accepted on the authority of the Church, including bishops like Augustine. This would no longer be the case. As a result, the Reformation still upheld foundationalism (i.e. basing one's beliefs on a foundation which is accepted uncritically), but there was a clear shift in the foundations. Rather than assert the authority and inerrancy of the Church, Protestants asserted the authority and inerrancy of Scripture, which was now made accessible to every believer (as much as possible). Indeed, Luther's stance was *sola Scriptura*, i.e. the assertion that Scripture alone is the rule of faith and conduct, and this likewise was a reaction against the interdisciplinary approach that was more characteristic of scholasticism and the Renaissance. Such foundationalism was a precursor to the fundamentalism of the early twentieth century.

CHAPTER 4

THE EARLY ENLIGHTENMENT

'Enlightenment' is a term that is applied rather broadly to the intellectual climate of the Western world from the seventeenth century into the twentieth century. In general, it marked a gradual shift away from foundationalism. As we saw in the previous chapter, this shift had already begun during scholasticism and the Renaissance. Foundations of knowledge were not abandoned altogether. Rather, the quest for certainty led thinkers to reject one type of foundation in favour of another. Over time this opened the door for postmodernism, which will be addressed more fully a little later. However, the process of questioning the sources of knowledge essentially created a wide spectrum of epistemic approaches, and all of these are still represented today in one form or another. It is likewise true that the ancient, medieval, scholastic, Renaissance and Reformation mindsets also exist today to some extent. Very seldom will a mindset disappear altogether, for it is highly likely that there will always be somebody who will embrace it. Furthermore, even when a particular mindset becomes rare in a culture, there are still multitudes of other cultures around the world where that mindset can find credence.

The best way to study periods of intellectual development is to address developments as they occur historically, analysing the way that different ideas are synthesized and developed. Thinkers are studied within their own context, and this not only includes recognizing cultural settings and historical events, but it also includes understanding the ways that thinkers serve as interlocutors with one another. Hence, intellectual history is often studied by closely examining the thought of figures who made key contributions to the overall developments that took place. This is certainly the best way to proceed, especially in dealing with a rather broad current like the Enlightenment. However, the constraints of time and space require a different approach, so in this chapter and the next I will again attempt to summarize the general developments, while noting the details that are most pertinent to the discussion which will ensue throughout the remainder of the book. Although several thinkers will be mentioned along the way, a number of other key figures will unfortunately go unmentioned. It is hoped that the interest of readers will be stimulated enough to generate further study with regard to these time periods and the intellectual developments that occurred within them.

RATIONALISM

Descartes (1596–1650) is often credited as being one of the founders of the Enlightenment, because he asked the sceptical questions that eventually led to the intellectual developments that emerged during this period. His quest was to attain certainty in knowledge, and he believed that a certain amount of scepticism is healthy, because this prompts us to examine the basis of our beliefs. Descartes concluded that the only real basis for certainty is the hypothesis 'I think, therefore I am.' In other words, since I can think, I must exist. Even if I am deceived in *what I am thinking about*, I cannot be deceived about *the fact that I am thinking*. For Descartes, this hypothesis is the basis of all other knowledge.

After speculating about the reliability of his senses and ability to reason, Descartes decided that they could be trusted, since God would neither deceive him nor leave him without the means to discovering the truth. However, he believed that logical reasoning can be trusted more than the senses, and he thus concluded that certain, reliable knowledge can be derived from clear, distinct perceptions. The most sound concepts are those that are pure, i.e. free from empirical conditioning. For example, Descartes agreed with the ontological argument for God's existence that was formulated by Anselm in the medieval period. In essence, the argument is that since God is by definition a perfect being, and since existence is necessarily a part of the concept of a perfect being, then it is logically contradictory to say that God does not exist. This argument has been controversial since its inception, and it has been criticized on several grounds.

Descartes' approach to knowledge is representative of what is referred to as *rationalism*. The basic assumption of rationalism is the reality of concepts which are not empirically conditioned. For many rationalists, the foundation for this is the existence of innate ideas which all human beings share in common. Innate ideas are certainly not based on experience in any way, so they can be neither established nor tested empirically. However, not all rationalists believe in innate ideas. These rationalists argue that there are still pure, non-empirical concepts which can be derived rationally from other concepts. According to this line of thinking, the best basis for knowledge is logical reasoning itself, and the most reliable concepts are those which are logically derived from pure concepts. Rationalism is most certainly the basis for idealism, and it can arguably be regarded as the forerunner of existentialism. We will examine these two movements shortly.

As I pointed out earlier, rationalism has its roots in the thought of Plato, and it continued to develop in the centuries that followed. Plato made a distinction between the eternal Forms (Ideas) and our temporally held concepts which only partially reflect them. Interestingly enough, this division has been appropriated in Christian thought throughout its history. For some, the division between the eternal and the temporal is wide, caused by the sin of humanity. They believe that human reason has been corrupted to the extent that knowledge of God (or other eternal or spiritual matters) cannot be ascertained through human reason. These concepts must be revealed supernaturally. Christians who adhere to this are not as sympathetic to rationalism (or many other types of epistemology), because they consider it presumptuous to base theological belief on human reasoning.

In contrast, other Christians do not view the division so sharply. They feel that some knowledge of spiritual things can be derived through natural reason, even though some things must still be supernaturally revealed. In fact, some Christian thinkers believe in innate ideas, especially common moral values. Christian rationalists try to derive theological beliefs from pure concepts (either revealed, discovered or innate) that are presumably not dependent on (sensory) experience. They attempt to prove propositions by using logical inference, and one of the most common instances of this is the law of contradiction, which is the methodology employed in the ontological argument. In other words, rationalists attempt to prove many things, not by constructing any positive basis for them, but by showing that since it is contradictory to deny these tenets, they must be true.

David Hume (1711–76) and Immanuel Kant (1724–1804) later attacked this tactic, especially in metaphysics (including religion). They pointed out that trying to prove a metaphysical proposition by the law of contradiction is highly questionable, to say the least, because the entire argument rests on the reliability of the concepts themselves. Since the concepts themselves are highly speculative, the assertions are even more speculative and are thus unreliable. For instance, how much can we say about the soul when we do not even know what it really is in the first place? An appeal can always be made to the teachings of Scripture to answer such questions, but this merely pushes the critical questions back to the issue of the authority (i.e. reliability) of Scripture itself. Of course, we could revert to foundationalism and uncritically accept the historically affirmed canon as fully inerrant, but how much certainty can this provide? If we desire something more, then other questions must be asked, and we will consider this a little later in the book.

EMPIRICISM

Just as rationalism can be traced back to Plato, empiricism is grounded in the thought of Aristotle. He claimed that all our knowledge originates in the senses, and this assertion is empiricism in a nutshell. In spite of its long history, empiricism has not always been championed. During the medieval period Aristotle's philosophy fell out of vogue, and empiricism was not strongly advocated. However, Aquinas helped to revive Aristotelianism in the thirteenth century, and empiricism eventually resurfaced during the Enlightenment. Descartes' writings certainly helped to spark interest in the subject, but the real tour de force of empiricism is John Locke's *Essay Concerning Human Understanding*, first published in 1689.

According to Locke (1632–1704), each of us is born with a mind that is like a blank slate. There are no such things as innate ideas. Some ideas merely seem to be innate because they are learned at such an early age. Moreover, the existence of pure (i.e. non-empirical) concepts is likewise a fiction. All our concepts, even the most complex ideas, are constructed from basic sense perceptions. For Locke, this essentially limits what can be regarded as meaningful language. He advocated a type of nominalism, claiming that we cannot speak of universal concepts, only particular things that we either experience or construct from our experiences. This claim was not novel, for the debate over nominalism had been rather heated during the late medieval period, the strongest proponent of nominalism being William of Ockham.

In Locke's mind, the reality of nominalism limits the credibility that can be given to testimony. The further removed testimony is from the actual event, the less reliable it is. We are susceptible to error even when we witness something first-hand. The more times a testimony is passed on, the greater the possibility of error becomes. Locke felt that this principle calls into question the reliability of Scripture, especially its claims about miracles like the resurrection of Christ. In the first place, we do not have the original documents of the New Testament, only copies of them. In the second place, the original documents themselves were written several decades after the event allegedly took place. The best thing to do, in Locke's opinion, is to evaluate the reasonableness of Scripture.

Locke's willingness to subject Scripture to scrutiny is definitely a turning point in history. A number of contemporary scholars characterize this shift as the subjection of Scripture to reason. However, I contend that this is a bogus claim, because Scripture had always been subject to reason, both in its canonization and in its interpretation. (I will say more about this later on.) In fact, all belief comes at the hands of reason, so it is not the case that Locke first placed Scripture in front of the judicial bench of reason. Rather, Locke changed the *criteria* by which Scripture would be evaluated. It was no longer sufficient to accept Scripture on the basis of the Church's claims of authority and infallibility. That had already been questioned and undermined. It was also unacceptable to base the authority of Scripture on circular arguments such as 'Scripture is inerrant because it is divinely inspired, and we know that it is divinely inspired because it tells us so.' The authority of Scripture would now need to be established on other grounds. In effect, Locke and other Enlightenment thinkers did not subject Scripture to reason for the first time. What they did was to use reason to erode the foundations on which the acceptance of Scripture had previously been based.

Empiricism in general opened the door for greater degrees of scepticism. There are three core elements of empiricism: 1) sensory perception; 2) concept formation; and 3) communication (so that we can benefit from the experiences of others). Any of these may be called into question. We might doubt the trustworthiness of our senses, the rationality of our thinking, or the effectiveness of the communication we have with others. Each of these was scrutinized in varying degrees throughout the Enlightenment, and attempts were made to salvage the certainty of knowledge in one way or another. Some were satisfied with these efforts while others delved into deeper scepticism. By the middle of the twentieth century, such scepticism had given rise to postmodernism, the most radical form of which denies the possibility of objectivity, certainty and substantive dialogue.

Consequently, postmodernism is not really antithetical to the Enlightenment. It merely takes the scepticism of the Enlightenment to higher (albeit not new) levels. For example, Hume had wondered whether an external world really exists or if the world were really a figment of his own imagination. After contemplating this dilemma, he decided that excessive scepticism (like that of the ancient Pyrrhonists) must be rejected, because we cannot function in that frame of mind. In short, we must trust our senses, because unless we are willing to do this, life becomes utterly perplexing and meaningless. Nevertheless, Hume still denied the possibility of miracles, and he basically rejected metaphysics as a whole.

This is not to say that empiricism necessarily leads to these higher degrees of scepticism. Many empiricists, e.g. scientists, place a great deal of confidence in our ability to perceive and analyse the world in which we live. To be sure, this confidence can be too great, and it is sometimes misplaced altogether. However, empiricists generally avoid making claims to absolute certainty, so this confidence is mediated to some extent. As a result, empiricists typically regard knowledge as *probable*, not certain. For most types of knowledge, regarding our beliefs as probable (and not certain) poses no real problems or threats for the vast majority of people. Of course, religious belief is another story altogether. Since religious beliefs are so important to us, many people are unwilling to hold them tentatively, and so they must defend their religious beliefs tenaciously and dogmatically.

Indeed, deep scepticism did not pervade empiricism. For instance, two notable attempts to maintain certainty in belief arose within empiricism itself. First, there were the common-sense realists. They maintained not only that the senses should be trusted, but also that the very foundations of all knowledge (including moral perceptions) cannot ultimately be scrutinized, because they are self-evident. Although some forms of common-sense realism were simplistic and naive, other forms like that promoted by G. E. Moore (1873–1958) were based on a rationale similar to Hume's rejection of excessive scepticism. Empiricists like Moore reasoned that if we deny the premises of knowledge, all statements are rendered useless and devoid of meaning. This precludes us from either making assertions or denying them. Nothing can be affirmed or rejected. In short, the attempt to deny the principles of knowledge is self-contradictory since it ends up undermining itself.

Second, some thinkers employed empiricist language metaphorically to account for the apprehension of realities and truths that they regarded as objective and transcendent. This was particularly true of a number of British empiricists in the seventeenth and eighteenth centuries. Francis Hutcheson, Joseph Butler and Anthony Ashley Cooper (Earl of Shaftesbury) were among those who asserted that we possess a 'moral sense' by which we perceive right and wrong. Along the same lines, theologians like Jonathan Edwards and John Wesley claimed that believers receive a 'spiritual sense' at conversion, and this allows the discernment of spiritual realities and truths. These appeals to extra 'senses' have much in common with the more naive versions of common-sense realism, because they allow ethical and metaphysical claims to be made and accepted uncritically. The use of empiricist terminology in these contexts is very deceptive, because even though our ethical and religious beliefs are based on perceptions, there is no way to prove that these perceptions are objective rather than subjective. (As we saw earlier, all perception involves interpretation, and this can be very subjective.) In addition, we trust our five senses because the perceptions we make from them are continually reinforced during our conscious moments. This kind of reinforcement cannot be claimed for our ethical and metaphysical beliefs.

METAPHYSICAL PERSPECTIVES

The questions of metaphysics (concerning the existence of anything beyond the material world) are as old as civilization itself. There are three basic positions regarding metaphysics. First, *dualism* is the belief in both material and transcendent (e.g. spiritual, eternal, intellectual) realms. Plato made a rather sharp divide between the material world and the eternal Ideas/Forms. For him death ultimately frees the soul from the prison of the body. Dualism was also the viewpoint of the New Testament writers, seen especially in the letters of Paul, which pit the spirit against the flesh and suggest that it is better to be absent from the body (i.e. dead) so that one can be in God's presence. When these two sources were integrated in the medieval period, it is not surprising that Christian thought during this time likewise regarded the material world as utterly corrupt and sinful, opposed to the spiritual sphere.

In time this view was rejected and the material world was regarded more favourably. However, this did not diminish the support for metaphysical dualism. Descartes continued the tradition by contending that the soul and the body interact in a small gland at the base of the brain. Gottfried Leibniz (1646–1716) later claimed that all things are comprised of minuscule, indivisible particles called monads, which contain both matter and spirit. In the meantime other versions of dualism have been proposed, and dualism has enjoyed a steady following all along.

The second metaphysical view is *materialism*, i.e. the belief that all that exists is matter. According to this view, things that are often considered to be transcendent (e.g. free will, soul) are really just complex physical realities. Consequently, materialists see the world in a very deterministic way. Everything can ultimately be explained by the laws of physics. Interest in materialism has obviously grown with the development of science, and this has caused many people to erroneously conclude that scientists are typically atheists and materialists. Granted, there are a few scientists who betray a bias against religion, perhaps even an agenda to discredit it altogether; nevertheless, objective scientists realize that science cannot make metaphysical assertions, since that lies beyond the empirical.

Unfortunately, too many see science as a threat to their religious beliefs. One reason for this is that they relegate religious belief to the realm of the unexplained. If science can explain how something happens, then there is no room for faith in God. Looking at the world in this way essentially makes religion and science mutual enemies, because each threatens to encroach upon the other's territory. For example, Sally recovers from cancer. If the doctors can explain how this happened, then she will regard it as a merely natural event. On the other hand, if her recovery defies explanation, then it must be an act of God. People like Sally live with these dilemmas because they believe that God acts *against* natural causes, rather than *through* them.

Since divine activity cannot be determined empirically, faith in supernatural assistance is by nature tentative. A number of people try to resolve this tension by gravitating towards one of two polar opposites. On the one hand, some simply regard everything as divine activity, and they see the world in a deterministic way. Everything that happens is a part of the divine will. On the other hand, others attribute very little, if anything at all, to supernatural intervention. During the early Enlightenment the Deists held such a view, proposing that God created the world to be self-governing and thus will not interfere with it.

Embracing a position between these opposites of determinism and naturalism requires us to admit that discerning divine activity in our daily lives is highly speculative. In fact, Locke coined the term 'enthusiasm' to describe those who mistake their own imaginations for the voice of God. Even theologians like Edwards and Wesley, who appealed to a 'spiritual sense' in believers, were concerned with this problem. Wesley preached a sermon and wrote several treatises on this topic, explaining how believers can have assurance of salvation without resorting to 'enthusiasm'. Edwards would not even condone a 'direct witness of the Holy Spirit' as Wesley did. In the end, both men tried to avoid fanaticism by formulating criteria by which religious experiences can be judged empirically.

Another reason that people consider science to be a threat to religion is the fact that their religious beliefs are based, at least in part, upon the historicity and authenticity of particular events. Of course, a threat is only perceived when: 1) there is fear that the historical basis might be invalidated; and 2) such invalidation is itself regarded as a threat to the religious beliefs in question. For instance, let us consider Marlene, who is a Latter Day Saint. If believing in the authenticity of the Book of Mormon is not a strong reason for her faith, then it will not disturb her if the text is called into serious question. If scholars debunk Joseph Smith's claim to have translated the text from golden plates that an angel revealed to him, she will not be alarmed or feel the need to reject the criticisms.

In contrast, if regarding the Book of Mormon as divinely inspired is important to Marlene, then she will be bothered by these attacks *if she suspects that there might be some truth to them*. Whatever objective confidence she might have in the authenticity of the texts will stem from a belief that the texts can withstand critical scrutiny. She might have confidence in the Book of Mormon based on a subjective 'burning in the bosom' that many LDS members claim, but this will not help her to face the critical issues. She would then have to either: 1) dismiss the critical scholarship out of hand; 2) give up her trust in the Book of Mormon; or 3) live with a serious gap in her belief structure.

Perceived threats such as these are not limited to science, but extend to all kinds of critical scholarship. Any attack on beliefs that are cherished yet vulnerable will cause alarm. Indeed, the feeling of alarm is dictated by the belief's importance and vulnerability, and the greater the claims made by the belief itself, the more vulnerable it will be. For instance, if charismatic Christians claimed that receiving the gift of tongues typically entails supernaturally speaking in one of the world's known languages, this belief would be rather easy to discredit. Charismatics usually make more modest claims, emphasizing the gift of tongues as supernaturally speaking in an ecstatic, unintelligible language which must also be interpreted supernaturally by another believer. The lesser claim is less vulnerable to critical scrutiny.

The final metaphysical perspective is *idealism*, which denies the reality of the material world. The idealist considers the transcendent realm (of spirit, thought, etc.) to be not just the ultimate reality, but the only reality at all. Two of the more famous accounts of idealism were those advanced by the Anglican bishop George Berkeley (1685–1753) and by the German philosopher Georg Wilhelm Friedrich Hegel (1770–1831). Writing at the time of ever-expanding scientific naturalism, both these men believed that their systems of thought preserved Christian belief from the kinds of criticism discussed above. Each version had its own emphases and its own set of problems. Berkeley's account was never really developed due to the dominance of empiricism in Great Britain. Hegel's philosophy was carried on for some time in what is known as German idealism, and it was developed and transformed in a number of ways, becoming the basis for several philosophies, including existentialism, phenomenalism and Marxism.

Idealism has never been sustained as a popular philosophy for any great length of time, and the main reasons for this are rather obvious. For one thing, idealism is unappealing because it is so abstract. Many prefer to think concretely, and some find it difficult to think abstractly for an extended period of time. More importantly, when idealism comes under the scrutiny of scepticism, it is difficult to avoid falling into solipsism, i.e. the belief that nothing exists beyond oneself. As I have already pointed out, even sceptics like Hume found this option unpalatable. In addition, idealism goes against our most basic intuitions, namely that we exist in a material world which we are able to perceive through our senses. All of that being said, the importance of idealism in intellectual history is not its own viability, but the fact that it helped to accelerate the already active trend towards subjectivism. We will focus more on this trend in the next chapter.

CHAPTER 5

THE BURGEONING OF THE ENLIGHTENMENT

The figure most often associated with the Enlightenment is Immanuel Kant, whose philosophy marked a monumental turning point in intellectual history. Thousands of books and articles have been written about him since he published the first of his critical works in 1781. Needless to say, Kant left an indelible mark on philosophy, ethics and religion, and much of the dialogue concerning epistemology during the past two centuries has either built upon or responded to Kant in some way. Of course, a significant portion of the response to Kant was also a reaction to Hegel, whose thought was a noteworthy and widely popular adaptation of Kant's philosophy. His first major work, *Phenomenology of Mind*, was published three years after Kant's death. In this chapter I will first sketch the major tenets of Kant's and Hegel's epistemology that are pertinent to religious epistemology, then we will briefly look at the principles of two key movements which followed – existentialism and pragmatism.

KANT

In his attempt to determine the limits of knowledge, Kant asserted that we cannot know things as they truly are (noumena), we can only know things as we experience them (phenomena). In other words, my ability to understand objects is limited to my ability to perceive through my senses. As I look at a tree in front of me, I can only speak of the tree as it appears to me. I can say how it looks, feels, smells, etc. However, it would be presumptive of me to claim that I experience the tree in every facet of its existence. This by no means suggests that the senses cannot be trusted, only that sensory perception cannot claim to be comprehensive, saying all that can be said about an object. In a nutshell, my understanding is limited by my ability to perceive through my senses.

A century earlier, Locke had proposed that when we experience objects, our minds form ideas that are essentially copies of these objects. He felt that our ideas are trustworthy because they conform to the objects that they represent, and this assumption was long shared by many. In fact, the common-sense realists trusted basic perceptions to the point of claiming that it is absurd to question or deny them. Before Kant entered the scene, it was generally believed that our ideas are determined by external objects. Kant rejected this and suggested the opposite, arguing that our ideas actually conform to our thought processes. (He regarded this thesis as revolutionary, similar to the scientific revolution started by Copernicus.)

Kant outlined what he considered to be the ways that our minds make sense of data. He was rather optimistic about most types of knowledge, because he did regard our ideas as reliable. He agreed with Aristotle that all our ideas originate with sensory experience, but he was somewhat Platonic in asserting that we can derive pure (a priori) concepts from empirical ones. According to Kant, we are able to do this by means of a set of concepts which are a natural and necessary part of reasoning itself, because we cannot make sense of experiences without them. The two most basic concepts in this list are space and time, but there are others as well, e.g. unity, existence and limitation. (In reality, Kant's list of categories was an expansion of Aristotle's categories.)

Nevertheless, Kant was influenced by the scepticism of Hume, and he was thus less optimistic about metaphysical concepts. He concluded that the only kinds of metaphysics of which we can be reasonably certain are things like pure mathematics, pure physics, and logic. Other types of metaphysics, including religion and morality, are speculative and cannot be demonstrated rationally. For instance, there is no way to determine whether I have a soul or not; it is mere conjecture. Likewise, although we can observe a certain order and harmony in the universe, at best this might suggest the existence of a Grand Designer, but this would not necessarily be an infinite God. (This was actually Hume's argument, and Kant concurred with it.) Kant did believe that if the universe does indeed have a grand design, its highest goal is the moral perfection of humanity. In his opinion, all human beings have a natural propensity and respect for morality, and he thus concluded that this is the best basis for religious concepts. It is religion that is dependent upon morality, not vice versa. Morality is helped by religious concepts, but its content is not determined by religion.

The relationship between morality and religion, as Kant envisions them, is rather intricate. To start, in order for morality to be sustained we must presuppose human freedom, an afterlife, and the existence of a God who will reward the virtuous in the afterlife. The latter presupposition is generally known as Kant's moral argument for God's existence. Additionally, he argued that religion, in its purest form, is essentially living a moral life as one's service to God – nothing more, nothing less. He considered Christianity to be morally superior to other religions, primarily due to the teachings and example of Christ. According to Kant, early Christianity had a clear emphasis on morality, but it soon became cluttered with unnecessary doctrines and hierarchy. Christians started to regard the practising of rituals and the reciting of creeds as that which pleases God, and Christianity consequently lost its moral focus. This interpretation of religion is reflected in much of the liberal Protestant theology which flourished in the late nineteenth and early twentieth centuries.

Kant's desire to establish the proper limits of knowledge is also reflected in what are called the antimonies. These are pairs of contradictory statements which can both be supported but not proved. Human freedom is perhaps the most familiar antimony. On the one hand, it seems that human choice is determined, because all our decisions are empirically grounded. In effect, our choices are not random, but are based on reasons that are ultimately empirical. On the other hand, it also seems that we have control over our decisions, that we can somehow transcend the influences which shape us without letting them determine us. In that way we have the ability to think and act freely. Kant's discussion of the antimony of human freedom reinforces his method of considering concepts from two perspectives – the transcendental and the empirical.

In the final analysis, Kant's thought represents a strong tension between optimism and scepticism. It is also a kind of synthesis between rationalism and empiricism, and this is also part of its beauty. These several innovations that Kant introduced paved the way for further developments, even entire systems of thought. Some regard Kant as an iconoclast, because he quickly dismissed claims to knowledge that he believed would not stand up to scrutiny.

However, Kant was as optimistic as he felt that he could be without compromising his intellectual integrity.

HEGEL

Hegel's transcendental idealism (mentioned at the end of the previous chapter) offered a notable reinterpretation of Kant. Hegel asserted that our concepts conform to objects, not to our patterns of thinking, as Kant suggested. Therefore, although Kant denied that we can know *things-in-themselves* (which is itself an abstraction), we can know *being* itself by understanding concepts. This begins with logic. However, it can allow no presuppositions. Rather, it starts with the notion of thought itself as pure being. This requires: 1) giving up the subjective point of view from which things are seen individually; and 2) thinking in an utterly passive way, allowing the concept to develop itself through analytic thinking.

In effect, although all things have particular characteristics that distinguish them individually, they all share one thing in common – being (i.e. existence). Contemplating being by itself is abstract and empty (i.e. devoid of all characteristics), so the thought of being is indeterminate and thus indistinguishable from the thought of nothing (i.e. sheer emptiness and indeterminacy). Nevertheless, the thought of nothing is also simple and immediate, and it thus turns back towards the thought of simple, immediate being. As a result, the thought of being and the thought of nothing, although distinct, tend towards one another. This tendency is *becoming*. In the final analysis, pure being is always becoming.

This insight gives rise to a dialectic in knowledge. Since all being necessarily has a negation (i.e. non-being or nothingness), knowledge occurs when a synthesis is formed between a thesis and its antithesis. Knowledge is thus a synthesis of: 1) the finite and the infinite; 2) the sensuous and the intelligible; 3) the necessary and the free; 4) the ideal and the real; and 5) idea and being. Consequently, the synthesis is Hegel's resolution of Kant's antimony. The dialectic actually lies beneath the unfolding of history, reflecting the general development of freedom towards self-consciousness.

Hegel essentially equated spirit and mind, and he believed that freedom is found in ideas. Each person is ultimately a transcendental, conscious self. Consequently, the act of knowing is consciousness simultaneously distinguishing itself from something while relating itself to it. Consciousness first perceives the object 'in-itself' (i.e. as it truly is). Then the object is altered for consciousness and perceived as 'being-for-consciousness of the in-itself'. In other words, even though we initially experience things as they truly are, we alter our perceptions of them somewhat in order to make sense of them. In the end, everything is essentially perceived from the perspective of the conscious self, not from any objective point of view. The self is conscious of itself through its ability to transcend and supersede external objects. The object is hence the negation of self-consciousness.

With regard to his views on religion, Hegel sounds very much like Spinoza (1632–77), who espoused a type of pantheism one and a half centuries earlier. (It also has strong similarities with Hinduism.) Spinoza had envisioned God as the sum total of all reality, an infinite substance with infinite attributes. According to Spinoza, God exists necessarily in everything. Other minds and things are merely finite modes of God. Hegel comes rather close to this, asserting the existence of an Absolute Mind/Spirit (*geist*), which we refer to as God. The Absolute Mind is essentially a type of cosmic consciousness that can only be known directly, not instrumentally or mediately.

Hegel suggests that the consciousness of the individual is an expression of Mind that is subjective, self-contained, self-related and free. Mind can also present itself objectively, taking the form of reality as an outside world. However, the highest form of Mind is when Mind becomes self-conscious. This starts with human beings first gaining self-consciousness, then becoming aware of God (i.e. Absolute Mind). Human awareness of the self and of the Absolute allows a dialectic to take place, and humans thus become aware of themselves as part of the Absolute. For Hegel, this recursion is in fact God's self-knowledge.

Although Hegel's transcendental idealism did not endure for a great length of time, it provided a baseline for other developments, all of which continued the trend towards subjectivity. Although Hegel believed in an Absolute, it was an abstract ideal which must be perceived subjectively. Furthermore, this concept is a clear departure from the conventional depiction of God as a personal being, and it shows up later in both Christian existentialism (e.g. Tillich's reference to God as the 'ground of all being') and process theology (which today is calling into question traditional notions of God as an infinite, immutable being). For the past three centuries philo-sophical and lay movements alike have continued to progress down the path to subjectivity. Interestingly enough, Hegel considered himself to be a defender of Christianity, protecting it from empirical attack. Making something more subjective will indeed protect it from outside attack, but it then loses some of its power to compel and obligate in the process.

EXISTENTIALISM

The emphasis on the self as free and self-determining was more fully developed in existentialism, so named because it starts with existence as the most basic reality. Building upon Hegel's understanding of exis-tence, existentialists emphasize the continual movement between 'being' and 'non-being', referred to as 'becoming'. Existentialists likewise analyse how 'doing' contributes to our 'being' and/or our 'becoming'. In spite of the varied perspectives that existentialism has produced, there has been one common thread – the stress on the need to realize and actualize one's 'true self'. This notion even shows up in some branches of psychology, e.g. Maslow's hierarchy of needs, which asserts that the highest and greatest human need is self-actualization.

Existentialism's popularity has largely been due to its emphasis on self-determination. It makes a sharp distinction between the inner conscious self and the external world. Existentialists believe that we do not need to be determined by our circumstances, for we can respond to them however we so choose. Our destiny is ultimately in our own hands. We are free to become our true selves if we so desire. However, not all existentialists share this confidence. Some do not believe that Hegel's dialectical method of synthesis really resolves Kant's antimonies. In fact, they believe that many (if not all) things in life are contradictory and cannot be resolved. They contend that much of life is an absurdity that we must learn to accept. We must 'embrace the nothingness', so to speak.

The development of existentialism likewise contributed much to an already increasing movement towards subjectivism. As founda-tionalism faded and empiricism gained a foothold, there was a growing emphasis on personal experience, since that is the basis of empiricism. Existentialism helped to catapult this subjectivism to new levels, because it placed truth above even the realm of empirical experience. For the existentialist, truth is subjective and starts with self-perception, not with perception of the outside world. Like Hegel, some existentialists still believe in some kind of objective truth and reality, but they feel that truth can only be grasped subjectively. Other existentialists are less optimistic, abandoning all belief in any objective truth or in any transcendent reality (e.g. God).

Existentialism epitomizes the advantages and disadvantages of subjectivism. On the positive side, subjectivism protects our beliefs from attack. Since our beliefs are not determined externally, they cannot be threatened externally either. Everything is what we choose to make it. We are free to be and do whatever we please. On the negative side, subjectivism breaks down dialogue and isolates people from one another, because it denies an objective frame of reference. Subjectivism also fails to give us any real confidence in our beliefs, because our beliefs cannot be tested or validated in any way. In the end, we can either revel in our freedom or lament the loss of meaning from our lives.

PRAGMATISM

In contrast with German idealism, which was propagated by the successors of Kant, a group of American thinkers founded a school of philosophy known as pragmatism, starting in the late nineteenth century. It is premised upon the notion that since truth is useful to us, the truth of a proposition can be identified by its practical value. The most familiar name among the pragmatists is perhaps John Dewey (1859–1952), whom we recognize as the 'Father of Modern Education'. However, the founding of pragmatism is generally credited to Charles Sanders Peirce (1839–1914). Peirce claimed that the overwhelming majority of disagreements that people have are due to a lack of clarity. Basically, he thought that all our beliefs can be reduced to simple statements about empirical observation and personal feelings. If we clarify our ideas, apparent discrepancies can be resolved.

Peirce also argued for a new type of reasoning called 'abduction'. Traditionally, two types of reasoning have been recognized. Deduction starts with a general premise (which is assumed), then it deduces specific things from the premise. An example of deductive reasoning is: 'God is perfect. Therefore God has perfect knowledge and perfect power.' The general assumption of God being perfect is the basis of asserting that God has specific types of perfection.

In contrast, induction takes specific observations and then integrates them into a general proposition. An inductive argument might run as follows: 'This vehicle has two wheels, two pedals, handlebars and a seat. Therefore it is a bicycle.' Deduction is more characteristic of rationalism, and induction is the general methodology in empiricism. As described by Peirce, abduction is in effect reasoning to the most reasonable explanation whenever a strictly logical inference cannot be made. A simple example of this would be concluding that it has rained based on the fact that the ground is wet. Although the ground could be wet for other reasons, rain seems to be the most likely (and logical) conclusion, even though it cannot be proved or even strictly inferred.

According to Peirce, this type of reasoning is routinely used by scientists in formulating hypotheses. First, an anomaly is observed, and an explanation is needed to account for it. Next, abduction is used to determine the most satisfactory possible explanation, and this becomes the hypothesis. After this, the hypothesis is tested inductively through the conducting of experiments. Last of all, the hypothesis is analysed deductively in order to confirm that the hypothesis will indeed predict the original anomaly. Induction and deduction essentially test what has already been asserted through abduction. In fact, it has been argued that intellectual progress cannot occur without abduction, since it is the only kind of reasoning which actually adds anything new. On the other hand, it can also be asserted that abduction is merely a 'looser' kind of induction, allowing broader inferences which might otherwise be excluded.

The scientific method is clearly favoured by Peirce. Indeed, some have averred that he was the first philosopher to elevate the scientific method to the status of an epistemological system. Peirce makes a case for the scientific method against the other ways that people generally establish their beliefs. The worst of these is what Peirce refers to as *tenacity*. This is a decision by the individual to simply believe something no matter what. A little better than this is believing something merely on the basis of *authority*, which generally maintains harmony through coercion. The other way that people fix their beliefs is through the *a priori* method. In this approach, people trust their natural inclinations and intuitions. Although this is preferable to the methods of tenacity and authority, it also falls short of the scientific method, the only method which adequately takes into account all the evidence that is available.

In spite of Peirce's intellectual accomplishments, he was not well known during his lifetime. It was his friend and colleague at Harvard, William James (1842–1910), who popularized pragmatism. However, James's rendition of pragmatism was considerably different from Peirce's account in several crucial respects. Peirce was not enthusiastic about James's developments, and he did not capitalize on the attention given to him due to James's popularity. Instead, he started referring to his own philosophy as *pragmaticism* to distinguish it from the work of James and Dewey.

The pragmatism of James was also a sharp reaction against the writings of William Kingdon Clifford (1845–79), a contemporary of James whose life ended prematurely due to tuberculosis. Clifford's well-known essay 'The Ethics of Belief' argues that it is always wrong to believe anything on insufficient evidence. This rather rigid empiricism essentially eliminates metaphysics from consideration and dismisses religious belief as chiefly a product of superstition. Clifford is not opposed to accepting things on the basis of authority per se, but we must have sufficient reason for trusting other sources in forming our beliefs.

James takes a more subjective approach to belief. He feels that we generally disbelieve all facts and theories for which we have no use. Something must have relevance before we will embrace it. However, there is often a lack of evidence to either support or refute many things that we must consider. In these instances, our 'passional nature' must choose between options when the choice cannot be made on intelligent grounds. This places belief between absolute certainty and scepticism. It is undesirable to claim that one truly knows something (with absolute certainty). However, being sceptical is also insufficient, because it is better to run the risk of committing error than it is to omit the truth. As a general rule, we believe that our precepts are shared in common with others, and this gives us confidence in our beliefs.

Consequently, moral and religious belief are decided by the will, since they are founded, at least in part, on non-empirical grounds. In James's opinion, even religious ideas like God, design and free will are only true to the extent that they have value for concrete life. Salvation itself is not necessary, but is probable nonetheless. Since the practical significance of concepts can vary depending upon the immediate circumstances, the truth value of the concepts varies as well. This yields a relativistic view of the universe, suggesting that the world is incomplete and subject to additions and subtractions. Indeed, James claims that knowledge grows in spots, like grease, as new experiences are related to old truths (i.e. beliefs). Through this process the world is constantly changing and improving.

In this schema truth is defined pragmatically. True ideas are those that we can assimilate, validate, corroborate and verify. James alleges that even transcendentalists (i.e. idealists, phenomenalists and existentialists) only regard their ideas to be self-transcendent because they find that their ideas do bear fruit. The truth of ideas is only revealed by their utility, but this is broader than narrow self-interest. Pragmatism does indeed start with the practical, but then it seeks to understand its theoretical foundation. It simply insists that truth should have practical consequences.

James also believes that religious phenomena are psychological and can be studied psychologically. The significance of any human event or condition must be judged empirically and religious experience is no exception. In fact, the same type of character that is produced by Christianity can be observed naturally. It is presumptive to claim any supernatural transformation of the psyche. If God's grace acts miraculously in the psyche, it probably does so subliminally, but this is indiscernible. Moreover, religious belief is speculative, according to James. In metaphysical and religious belief, reasons are only cogent if we are already influenced by feelings. In other words, it is instinct that leads, intelligence merely follows. (This is a restatement of Hume's earlier claim that reason always is and ought to be the slave of the passions.) For James, feeling is the deeper source of religion. Philosophical and theological formulas are secondary byproducts. Religious beliefs are ultimately reinforcements of our demands on ourselves and on one another. Indeed, once people are convinced of something on the basis of subjective reasons, they will not be convinced by objective reasons.

Nevertheless, James concludes that religion is necessary for living a full life. The vulnerability of saintliness is generally necessary for social evolution. Religious virtues thus promote the advancement of society. Since belief in the absolute places rigorous ethical demands on us that we cannot meet, it must necessarily offer salvation to us. This provides us with 'moral holidays' in which we live by grace rather than by law. In general, believing in an absolute reality is generally a way to cope with the difficulties of life, not a means of making it more complicated.

Obviously, James made pragmatism much more subjective, basing belief more on feelings, not on the scientific method as Peirce had done. Both these strands of pragmatism are still evident today. However, Peirce's emphasis on the scientific method probably does not extend very far beyond the scientific community. In contrast, James's more popularized version can be seen in religious circles and in society at large. It reinforces the natural human tendency to base belief on personal relevance and benefit. In other words, we are quick to embrace or reject beliefs that we consider to be personally relevant. However, if we deem particular beliefs to be inconsequential to our own lives, then we will not be motivated to embrace or reject them. It is indeed rare to meet people who care very deeply about matters that do not impact on them personally in some way. As we have already noted, this is due to the fact that all motivation is grounded in self-interest, and it is thus difficult to maintain broad reasons for believing and acting and not to allow our reasons to become narrow.

CHAPTER 6

MORE RECENT DEVELOPMENTS

In this section of the book I have endeavoured to give a general overview of intellectual history, which I believe will provide us with a good frame of reference throughout the remainder of the book. As history has unfolded and new developments have arisen, older views by and large have been replaced, but never completely. As a result, all the views from the past are ostensibly still represented to some degree. Some of the more antiquated ways of viewing the world have continued to flourish, but this has often required them to be changed and adapted to new circumstances. Consequently, the intellectual state of society at any given point in time is a complex mixture of perspectives from the past. The fact that intellectual progress and cultural development have not occurred uniformly throughout the world has only added to the complexity. Obviously, recent developments are more likely to have strong support, but this does not indicate their long-term viability.

In this chapter we will reflect on the impact of fundamentalism, logical positivism and postmodernism during the past century. Although logical positivism died off due to its lack of success, fundamentalism and postmodernism are polar opposites which continue to wield great influence today. However, we must keep in mind that not everyone is either a fundamentalist or a postmodernist, because various perspectives from the past are still represented, some in great numbers. Nevertheless, these two movements have been so pervasive that most people have had to respond to them in some way.

FUNDAMENTALISM

The advent of fundamentalism was primarily occasioned by the escalation of two intellectual projects. First, biblical scholarship began focusing on what is known as *modern higher criticism*. For many centuries, scholars had been engaged in lower criticism, which involves scrutinizing the texts of Scripture in order to determine the most likely wording of the original documents, which we do not have. This is accomplished by comparing the copies that we have to one another (since there are differences in all of them). Lower criticism admits that there may be errors in our copies of Scripture, but it rests on the assumption that the original documents are divinely inspired, and for many Christians this has historically entailed the belief that the original texts are inerrant or at least infallible. The majority of Christians today are willing to accept new translations of Scripture, including the textual corrections that have been made by scholars, because lower criticism does not necessarily threaten even the highest view of scriptural inspiration (i.e. inerrancy).

Modern higher criticism, for all intents and purposes, calls into question these high views of scriptural inspiration, because it critiques the content of the original documents themselves. For instance, books like *Life of Jesus* by David Friedrich Strauss and *Quest for the Historical Jesus* by Albert Schweitzer cast doubt on the historical accuracy of the Gospels. Numerous other studies have raised similar questions about the Bible, such as: 1) Were the books actually written by the supposed authors?; 2) What sources were used in writing them?; 3) Do they conflate or exaggerate the narratives in any way?; 4) What were the agendas of the authors?; and 5) To what extent were the authors influenced by the religions, cultural customs, and philosophies of the ancient Near East? All these questions cast doubt on the inerrancy of Scripture, regarding the texts first and foremost as human products.

The interesting thing is that the reaction against modern higher criticism spilled over into the rejection of lower criticism as well. Centuries earlier, the Protestant Reformation had enabled people to translate the Bible into various languages, and this resulted in disputes over the worth of particular translations. After all, since Protestants had discarded the Catholic belief that the Church (hierarchy) interprets Scripture without error, they had to place their trust in the integrity of the text itself, which they began to regard as inerrant. Consequently, people took the translation of Scripture very seriously, and they were rather adamant in endorsing particular translations.

The King James Bible was translated in 1611 to help end much of the bickering for the English-speaking people, and this became the standard English translation. The masses became so accustomed to using this translation that it started to be regarded as inerrant, too. (I once heard someone actually assert that the King James Bible was 'God's gift to the English-speaking world'.) As modern higher criticism emerged, archeologists were also unearthing older manuscripts of Scripture which had some notable discrepancies with the 'Textus Receptus' ('Received Text'), i.e. the documents which had been used for the King James Bible. Newer translations were produced, taking these discrepancies into account, and many inerrantists saw this as another 'modernist' attack on the Bible.

The second occasion for the advent of fundamentalism was the spread of the theory of evolution at the end of the nineteenth century. Many of the inerrantists were (and still are) biblical literalists, i.e. people who believe that the Bible must be interpreted literally whenever possible. Of course, literalists never extended this to the entirety of Scripture, because some writings (especially in the prophetic books) were obviously intended by the authors to be understood symbolically. For the vast majority of the inerrantists, historical passages could never be interpreted metaphorically. Events were intended to be taken literally.

Notwithstanding these limitations, a few fundamentalist figures, like the Princeton theologian Benjamin Warfield, were willing to interpret the seven days of creation metaphorically if this could still include the creation of an actual Adam and Eve. In other words, Warfield was open to the possibility of evolution so long as it could be believed that it resulted in an original pair of human beings. Most fundamentalists were not conciliatory at all, for they could not reconcile evolution with their literal, inerrantist understanding of Scripture.

Besides the threat to inerrancy, evolution also posed some difficulties for several key traditionally held Christian beliefs. Christians had long accepted the narrative regarding the transgression of Adam and Eve as a historically accurate account of the origins of human sinfulness. According to this interpretation, God created the world in a pristine state, then Adam and Eve corrupted themselves and the rest of creation through their own sin. God gave Adam and Eve freedom, because their love for God and their obedience to God would be empty and meaningless if not freely chosen. This freedom is what allowed the possibility of sin. In this regard, Christians have historically disagreed as to whether sin (as understood in this schema) was inevitable. However, it has generally been asserted that the sin of Adam and Eve corrupted human nature, and this corruption is transmitted from parent to child. This is the traditional doctrine of original sin. It blatantly overlooks the philosophical problems internal to the text itself, especially the supposition that God created two adults possessing developed reasoning and language without conditioning their behaviour in any way.

The theory of evolution directly challenges this. There was no pristine state according to evolution. Rather, good and evil increased gradually alongside one another as concomitants of the development of freedom. This is basically the theory offered by theistic evolutionists (i.e. those who regard evolution as the means by which God created the world). Whereas the traditional doctrine of original sin lays the entire responsibility for sin on human beings, theistic evolution regards evil as a natural by-product of the development of good, since both are rooted in rational (rather than instinctive) choice. Nevertheless, understanding creation within an evolutionary framework still requires the 'survival of the fittest', and many Christians find this loathsome.

Fundamentalists object to evolution on various grounds. Some argue that evolutionists are all atheists who want to destroy Christianity and the Bible. Although there are certainly some evolutionists who exhibit a definite antagonism against religion, this is by no means widespread. Scientists thrive on challenging and disproving existing theories, since this establishes their importance in their respective fields. Indeed, many scientists realize that science cannot ultimately speak about values and metaphysics, because science is an empirical enterprise and cannot address non-empirical matters like values and metaphysics. Rather, science merely informs the values and beliefs that we hold.

Other fundamentalists debunk the scientific methods used by evolutionists, but these attacks are often bogus, because they depend upon an extreme scepticism that fundamentalists would never impose on their own beliefs. Moreover, such scepticism would essentially undermine much of what we claim as knowledge. Fundamentalists also rely on their own alternative theories regarding the fossil record, but these are only embraced by those whose agenda is just as strong and biased as the atheists they decry.

At its heart, fundamentalism is a defensive, polemical stance. The first strands of fundamentalism were attempts to make an intellectual defence against 'modernism' (especially modern higher criticism and evolution). The main goal was to define 'the fundamentals' of Christianity. In reality, such efforts to define what is to be regarded as legitimate are actually attempts to eliminate undesirable elements. The identification of 'the fundamentals' was not a simple distinction between essentials and non-essentials. Instead, it was the rejection of those who did not accept 'the fundamentals', and this obviously rules out biblical critics and evolutionists.

Fundamentalists like Warfield represent the more intellectual strand of fundamentalism, and this type of fundamentalism is becoming increasingly prominent. There are certainly fundamentalist scholars who forge rather sophisticated arguments, but these hypotheses are still nothing more than mere apologetics. Fundamentalists refuse to ask the critical questions and to address the critical issues. Instead, they either start with a comfortable foundation and argue from that, or they try to support their assertions by undermining competing claims. Fundamentalist scholars will often limit their research to 'safe' areas where their rudimentary beliefs will not be challenged. For example, biblical scholars can focus on word studies and theologians can focus on historical studies. Critical disciplines like systematic theology and philosophy are avoided, and those who do participate in them do so from a polemical, apologetic stance. Of course, fundamentalists can also become very learned in other disciplines of knowledge without threatening their religious beliefs.

Nevertheless, another broad strand of fundamentalism exists. It is anti-intellectual altogether, dismissing all forms of critical scholarship out of hand. To be sure, the anti-intellectual fundamentalists generally value the scholarly fundamentalist apologists, because this polemical research reinforces their beliefs and makes them feel intellectually informed. However, there are some fundamentalists who do not even value the scholarly apologetics. They eschew anything rational or intellectual, and they insist that the Christian life has little or nothing to do with thinking. They rely on their own feelings and intuitions instead.

Fundamentalism suffered embarrassment after the 1925 Scopes trial over the teaching of evolution in US public schools. As a result, a number of conservative Protestants began identifying themselves as 'evangelicals' in order to distance themselves from the fundamentalists. Evangelicals considered themselves successors to the likes of Jonathan Edwards, John Wesley, Charles Finney and D. L. Moody. The two major assertions of evangelicalism are: 1) the authority of Scripture; and 2) the need for a personal conversion in order to be a Christian. These evangelicals wanted to be seen as conservative, yet open-minded, not dogmatic like their fundamentalist counterparts.

In the late 1970s and early 1980s Jerry Falwell and his organization, the Moral Majority, brought fundamentalism back into vogue for a short time. People were once again proud to be identified among the ranks. Nevertheless, the popular press effectively sullied the term once again by equating it with religious extremism. Fundamentalists began to hide behind the less offensive term 'evangelical', and so many so-called evangelicals today are actually covert fundamentalists. (It is also interesting to note that some moderate theologians and ethicists also now identify themselves as evangelicals, because they stress the need to obey the Gospel.)

LOGICAL POSITIVISM

The term 'positive philosophy' was coined by Auguste Comte in the nineteenth century. He also coined the term 'sociology', and he is generally regarded as the father of modern sociology. Comte believed that social progress has historically taken place in three phases, and this progression can be observed in every discipline of science. Before the Enlightenment was the *theological phase*, in which social relationships were defined as matters of duty to God. The Enlightenment ushered in the *metaphysical phase*, and this emphasized universal duties and rights as the guides of society. Comte called the final period the *scientific phase* or the *positive phase*. He felt that after the failure of the French Revolution and the subsequent defeat of Napoleon, the notion of universal rights had become obsolete and could now be replaced with a more scientific understanding of society. This new model is based on positive philosophy, so called because it does not resort to imaginary concepts for its justification. Rather, it strictly limits evidence to empirical data.

It is positive not only in reference to the certainty that can be obtained through it, but also with respect to its potential for promoting intellectual progress.

Building upon Comte's positive philosophy, the movement known as logical positivism began in the 1920s with a group of scholars known as the Vienna Circle. Their ranks included notable figures like Moritz Schlick, Rudolph Carnap and Otto Neurath. This movement spread rapidly throughout Europe and the US, making its greatest impact in the philosophy of science. The person usually credited with introducing logical positivism to Great Britain is the famous empiricist A. J. Ayer, who is a pivotal figure in the development of postmodernism.

According to logical positivism, there are only two types of meaningful statements: tautologies and empirical observations. Technically speaking, the two types are analytic a priori and synthetic a posteriori statements. This nomenclature harks back to Kant, who made two distinctions regarding concepts. First, concepts can be either analytic or synthetic. In analytic concepts, the predicate is contained within the subject. For example, 'All circles are round' is an analytic statement, because the concept of roundness is part of the concept of a circle. Synthetic concepts are formed when different elements are synthesized to form the predicate. An example of this would be 'John is taller than Bill.' This concept is formed from the concepts of John's height, Bill's height, and tallness itself.

Second, Kant said that concepts can be either a priori or a posteriori. A priori concepts are not dependent on experience in any way, because they are always true. For instance, 'The sum of the interior angles of any triangle is 180 degrees' is a priori, since it is true for any triangle whatsoever. In contrast, a posteriori concepts depend upon experience, for they are only circumstantially true. For example, 'Sally's car is red' is a posteriori, since this determination can only be made by looking at the car. It is not necessary that Sally's car is red, for her car may be any number of colours. It just happens to be the case that Sally's car is red, and this must be empirically observed.

Kant took these two distinctions and constructed a grid from them. Analytic a priori concepts are necessarily true, because the predicate is contained in the subject. This category includes such things as the laws of both logic and physics. Synthetic a posteriori concepts are constructed from empirical observations. Kant concluded that analytic a posteriori concepts are not possible, because the predicate cannot be contained in the subject and still be dependent on experience. However, Kant did believe that synthetic a priori concepts are possible. These are concepts that we must construct synthetically, yet they are not dependent upon how we experience them. In other words, they are necessarily true, but we cannot access them directly, and must construct them.

This category is where we find metaphysics, including religious concepts. For example, the concept of God would by definition be independent of experience, but we must construct it from other concepts. This is why the concept of God is essentially analogical (i.e. 'God is like . . .'). Kant thus regarded many traditional notions about God to be nothing more than anthropomorphism, i.e. they project human qualities onto the concept of God, even though this cannot be done rationally. Consequently, although Kant believed that these concepts are possible, he felt that they are highly speculative by nature.

The logical positivists were more sceptical than Kant, and so they dismissed synthetic a priori concepts categorically. They believed that the other two categories are the only legitimate ones, and these reduce all meaningful statements to tautologies and empirical observations. A statement like 'Every dog is an animal' is a tautology, because it asserts nothing new. The concept of animal is a part of the concept of dog. All new assertions are ultimately grounded in empirical observation. We can make statements about what we experience through our senses, and this adds new information to the mix.

The logical positivists felt that they had effectively eliminated metaphysics. Religious statements and other assertions about any transcendent or ultimate reality are empty and meaningless. They are nothing more than expressions of our personal feelings. (This claim had been made in the nineteenth century by several thinkers, including Feuerbach and Marx.) If I claim that there is a God, I am actually saying that it brings me pleasure to believe that there is a God. In fact, metaphysical claims in general are mere conjecture, since they are not empirically based.

This exposes the true nature of logical positivism. It is simply a stricter form of empiricism, because it recognizes only empirical observation as a legitimate source of knowledge. The logical positivists were optimistic that their project would lead to establishing the certainty of knowledge. They felt that if everything were founded on empirical observations and constructed logically, then certainty could be achieved. Notwithstanding their efforts, the project ultimately failed. In the first place, logical positivism not only precluded metaphysics, it also ruled out scientific theories, since they cannot be strictly inferred, but are somewhat speculative. It was clear that logical positivism had eliminated too much. In addition, some still refused to give up on the possibility of metaphysics. Others took matters even further by questioning the objectivity and reliability of human reason and sensory perception, and this ushered in postmodernism.

POSTMODERNISM

There is currently a more general intellectual trend known as postmodernism, so called because many regard it as the end of the modern period (a.k.a. 'modernism' or 'modernity'). It signifies the utter rejection of foundationalism. In essence, the postmodernist does not accept any real foundations for knowledge. Nothing is taken for granted or affirmed uncritically. As such, postmodernism questions all authority. Furthermore, it asserts that there are no absolute values or meaning, or it at least claims that we cannot apprehend any absolutes, even if they do exist. All value and meaning for the postmodernist are relative.

As a direct consequence of this scepticism, a number of postmodernists aver that all discourse breaks down at some point. In the first place, there is no foundation on which dialogue can take place. Additionally, the communication of ideas is illusory, because our use of words is personal and does not match the way others use the same words. When two people speak of the same thing, there is no way to determine exactly what the other person means. Moreover, since we cannot make sense of life from some objective perspective (because none exists), we construct our own 'metanarratives' which simply tell our life stories from our own individual perspectives. At best, metanarratives can intersect. My 'story' can connect with your 'story' in some way. However, we likewise each perceive these intersections from our own subjective point of view.

All this has impacted religious belief and belief in general. According to postmodernism, everything must be personally relevant, because that is the only relevance we can determine anyway. Truth itself is fully relativized. There is no objective frame of reference, so truth is limited to the coherence of our own beliefs. (More will be said about this later.) In short, postmodernism is the completion of subjectivism. It carries Enlightenment scepticism to great lengths, stopping just short of nihilism (i.e. the denial of everything).

CONCLUSION

Throughout history the pendulum of belief has swung back and forth between optimism and pessimism (i.e. scepticism), and it will most likely continue to do so in the future. Many buy into post-modern relativism, and others recoil from it completely, resorting to a dogmatic absolutism. Some Christian authors have accepted post-modernism and have concluded that the best thing is to temper it through the construct of community. They utilize virtue theory to support their view that Christianity need only be propagated as the heritage of particular Christian traditions. This merely attempts to reconcile personal faith with historic Christianity and legitimize the numerous Christian sects and denominations. It is simply a some-what lower level of subjectivism that still falls back on tradition as a foundation.

There has been another recent response to postmodernism that offers both appeal and promise – postfoundationalism. In this approach, foundationalism is rejected, but foundations are not dis-carded altogether. Instead, the foundations themselves must be scru-tinized and are thus subject to revision. Postfoundationalism takes seriously the issues raised by both the Enlightenment and postmod-ernism. The subjectivity of thought and discourse are recognized, but this does not necessitate lapsing into utter relativism. Rather, human rationality is regarded as an evolutionary device of survival. In this way, no particular type of epistemology can claim dom-inance, but different realms of knowledge (including science and religion) are actually part of the larger quest for meaning. This approach claims to avoid the pitfalls of foundationalist objectivism and postmodernist subjectivism.

SECTION THREE

CONSTRUCTING BELIEF

CHAPTER 7

THE BASIS OF BELIEF

The focus of the book will now turn back to belief itself. We will investigate various aspects of belief in order to evaluate the quality of particular beliefs. The obvious place to start is with the basis of belief. Belief is fundamentally a type of judgement, an exercise of reason. The opening chapters of the book discussed the basic dynamics of belief, and there we observed that people embrace beliefs for a number of reasons. People do not always believe things because they are convinced deep down that these things are true. Such inconsistencies and inadequacies in belief can cause gaps in the overall belief structure, and these should be eliminated or reduced whenever possible.

However, it is clearly better to believe something because we are convinced of its truth. It is not a mere coincidence that the word 'true' means both 'accurate' and 'trustworthy', and this association is certainly relevant to belief. The more accurate our beliefs are, the more we are able to trust them. Consequently, the value of belief is greatly determined by our ability to determine how true or untrue something may be. Therefore, we should take a moment to examine the nature of truth itself.

TRUTH

There are three prominent theories regarding the nature of truth. First, the *correspondence theory* asserts that something is true to the extent that is corresponds with reality. For example, the statement 'Abraham Lincoln was assassinated in Ford's Theater' is true because the meaning conveyed by it corresponds with historical facts. The second theory of truth is the *coherence theory*. According to this theory, propositions are not true individually. Rather, truth is the property of a group of propositions, namely its coherence. In effect, good beliefs fit together consistently and harmoniously. The third theory regards belief as true inasmuch as it is useful. This is the *pragmatist theory* of truth.

The coherence and pragmatist theories are both subjective, and so they suit postmodernism quite nicely. The fact that beliefs are coherent does not make them objectively true. Many outdated scientific theories were coherent, but they were eventually refuted or replaced. In a similar fashion, my mother's explanations about Santa Claus were certainly coherent, but they were not grounded in reality, only loosely constructed from it. The pragmatist theory is also subjective, because the usefulness of a belief at best indicates its truth *in the circumstances in which it is useful*. Suppose a man has an undetected heart condition in which strenuous activity could be dangerous. After playing a game of tennis, he feels very well, enjoying the exercise. He believes that his heart is healthy, for his athletic performance was better than expected. He decides to play again the following week, but the result is very different. He drops dead, the victim of a heart attack. His belief that his heart was not in any danger was arguably useful in the first game, but it clearly was not in the second. As such, it could be said that from the perspective of the first game his belief was true. Nevertheless, his belief was not objectively true, so it was irrelevant beyond that set of circumstances.

In contrast, the correspondence theory is objective, since it bases truth on the objective reality of facts. If this theory is valid, then we can discover truth that transcends particular circumstances. Granted, things correspond with one another in varying degrees, so although the correspondence theory is objective, it still allows for degrees of truth. For instance, the statement 'Abraham Lincoln was stabbed in Ford's Theater' is partially true and partially false. Even though the statement is not entirely true, the truth within it is objective. Lincoln was indeed killed in Ford's Theater, but was shot.

However, before the correspondence theory can be adopted, we must answer postmodernism's question as to whether there is an objective frame of reference in the first place. If there is, then the correspondence theory will be the most valuable of the three, because it can be extended beyond particular circumstances. If there is not, then the correspondence theory will be irrelevant. Of course, there is always a subjective frame of reference in every given instance, so the coherence and pragmatist theories always have some validity. Nevertheless, they cannot be extended more broadly. Coherent beliefs cannot necessarily be related to beliefs outside the system, and pragmatic beliefs cannot be trusted beyond the circumstances in which they are useful.

OBJECTIVITY

Everything that we perceive is understood from our own subjective perspective. Consequently, there is no way to prove absolutely that there is an objective frame of reference. Notwithstanding this difficulty, we believe that there is one. We cannot relate to the external world otherwise. We rightly believe that others experience the same things that we do. The more that this seems to be the case, the more convinced we become that there is objectivity. In other words, although an objective frame of reference cannot be proved or intuited (i.e. known directly), it does not need to be merely assumed, because its existence is continually made manifest in our lives. Our life's experiences establish over time our belief in objectivity.

Consider the case of dementia. Mental illness can cause people to 'see' and 'hear' things that are not really there. Such sufferers become isolated from others, because their 'experiences' are unique to them alone, not shared by others. This leaves them with only two options. They can either trust themselves and mistrust others, or vice versa. Either way, the basis for any belief in objectivity is shaky at best. There must be some consistency in one's experiences (both internally and with the reactions of others) before there can be a solid basis for objectivity. Otherwise, life does not make sense.

The real problem is not with objectivity itself, but with our ability to distinguish objectivity within our beliefs, since we perceive everything subjectively. Many people wrongly conclude that beliefs about objectivity are themselves fully objective. For example, the religious assertion 'I believe in absolute truth' is still made from a subjective point of view. There may indeed be absolute truth, but this does not make my perceptions of it *absolutely true*. We routinely have subjective beliefs about objective realities. For instance, the belief that the earth is flat is certainly focused on an objective reality (the earth), but the perspective (flatness) is subjective. We know that the earth is spherical because our perspective has been broadened. Hence, we can increase the objectivity of our beliefs by broadening our perspective. Too many people live in the same 'box' for all of their life, and they remain blind to the limitations of their own beliefs.

In the final analysis, there are plenty of reasons for believing in objectivity, so the correspondence theory is certainly relevant. We can determine the truth of something by judging how much it corresponds with reality. However, we must recognize our own epistemic limitations. We are not omniscient, but are always susceptible to error. Moreover, there is no completely objective frame of reference from which we can make judgements. Intellectual maturity thus requires epistemic humility which is neither overly confident nor overly sceptical. Although there are seemingly very few things of which we can be absolutely sure (perhaps none at all, given our limitations), we still believe many things to be true because there is sufficient reason to affirm them. We put our trust in them because we consider them to be reliable. Consequently, the reliability of our beliefs aids us in determining their truth value.

RELIABILITY

We rely on beliefs all the time. For example, we all believe that the sun will come up tomorrow. Hume argued that we cannot be absolutely certain of this, since tomorrow may be the exception to the trend. He thus felt that causation is somewhat illusory, because at best it can only be inferred. Hume's view is accurate inasmuch as future events can be neither proved nor predicted with absolute certainty. However, belief in causation is justified when we consider the matter in terms of reliability. The sun does indeed come up every day, and this gives us great reason to believe that it will come up tomorrow as well. Moreover, our understanding of gravity, the earth's rotation, etc. only adds to the reliability of this belief. As such, we can trust it, and since everyone else trusts it, too, we can also regard it as a true, objective belief.

Reliability is a good means of assessing the solidity of a belief. It takes into account both the objective and the subjective elements of belief. This is why it is generally rejected by extremists on both sides of the spectrum. Those who claim that belief and truth are merely subjective feel that reliability cannot really be determined or asserted. In contrast, those who claim absolute certainty in their beliefs do not embrace concepts like reliability, because they acknowledge the subjective element of belief. Indeed, something can either be more narrowly and immediately reliable, or it can be more universally and broadly reliable. Reliability can be established both subjectively and objectively.

The example given above demonstrates two basic ways of establishing reliability. First, a belief becomes more reliable as we understand why it is reliable. We believe that the sun will come up tomorrow because we have some insight as to why this will be the case. We are aware of some of the details as to how the sunrise takes place. Second, a belief becomes more reliable as it is tested. With every passing sunrise, we have greater reason to believe that the trend will continue. Moreover, we can even test our theories regarding the sunrise. In a nutshell, reliability is established through both justification and verification. Whenever justification is made on theoretical grounds, it tends to be more objective than verification, provided that speculation is kept to a minimum. After all, theories represent our attempts to summarize a range of experiences, and they are more reliable when they depend upon a broader range of observations in their formation. The broader the range, the more objective they are.

A belief is also deemed to be more reliable as it is verified. In contrast with justification, verification establishes reliability more practically, because it does not necessarily require further theorizing. It simply tests the belief in question. In our example, observing the sunrise each day accomplishes this. However, verification can also test the theories employed. For instance, we can verify our theories regarding the motion of the earth around the sun. Of course, this is also limited to our ability to observe and interpret our observations. After all, Galileo was unable to verify his theory (about the earth orbiting around the sun) because he could not make use of satellite photos. The most sophisticated piece of equipment at his disposal was a telescope.

JUSTIFICATION

Even though beliefs can be justified in a number of ways, several criteria are crucial to making a thorough assessment. To start, the *basis* of the belief must be evaluated. *What are the premises of the belief? What assumptions have been made?* Beliefs can only be as strong as the foundations on which they rest. If these foundations are faulty or weak, then the belief cannot be justified sufficiently.

Next, the *rationale* of the belief needs to be identified and analysed. *Is the reasoning logical? Are other assumptions being made along the way?* A belief may start with a sold basis but then make huge jumps as it takes shape. This weakens the belief. The tighter (i.e. more logical, less speculative) the reasoning, the more stable the belief will be.

Another important criterion to assess is *coherence*. Each belief must be coherent within itself, and all beliefs should fit into a coherent system. Inconsistencies basically indicate faulty reasoning and/or incompatible premises. We cannot make conflicting assumptions and then expect our beliefs to be coherent.

Last of all, we should also assess the *comprehensiveness* of our beliefs. As we have already noted, this is essentially one of several ways to determine the objectivity of our beliefs. The more comprehensive our beliefs are, the more useful they will be, both to us and to others on whom our lives make some kind of impact. It is much easier to have solid, coherent beliefs within a very limited range of circumstances. However, the more information that our beliefs take into account, the more difficult the task becomes.

VERIFICATION

The primary way to verify beliefs and hypotheses is to do it practically by conducting a series of tests. A number of people assert that religious beliefs cannot be assessed in any other way. We must simply put our faith in them and see if they 'work'. Whenever this is the primary basis for accepting beliefs, it essentially entails embracing the pragmatist theory of truth. In other words, if we believe certain things simply because they 'work' for us, then we adopt a rather subjective view of truth in which things are judged according to their relative usefulness in our lives (and in the lives of those around us). This is pragmatism at its finest, a very subjective approach to belief.

Nevertheless, testing our beliefs practically is certainly necessary, because many times extraneous factors and details are overlooked at the theoretical level. Something may sound good 'on paper', but it may not work in practice. This may indicate that the theory is wrong, but it may also be due to the fact that something significant has been missed along the way. Unlike many of his predecessors and contemporaries, John Wesley felt that religious beliefs must be tested practically. He believed that if doctrine is correct, then it should be confirmed by experience. On the other hand, if experience contradicts our doctrines, then the doctrines are probably faulty at some point. Wesley thus nuanced and altered his views throughout the course of his life. Unfortunately, Wesley's successors gave too much place to experience in forming religious beliefs, and they engaged in what they called 'experimental theology', an approach that truly represents the subjective pragmatism described above. Figures like Wesley were often cited by those who attempted to justify the rising tide of subjectivism, which could not be stemmed.

Beliefs can also be verified theoretically. This is different from justification. Whenever a belief is justified, its theoretical support and rationale are evaluated. Beliefs are verified theoretically by applying them to hypothetical examples. In science, theories are often tested by seeing how well they can handle 'boundary/border cases'. For example: is the universal law of gravitation relevant in a black hole? In essence, the limits of theories are determined by identifying the range of their applicability. Ethicists likewise use hypothetical situations to determine how far moral principles can be obeyed without disrupting other moral sensitivities. For instance, the belief that killing is wrong is accepted almost universally, but many people would indeed consider taking the life of another in dire circumstances. Some would go to war, others might protect their families through the necessary use of force, and others would likely intervene if someone were being murdered in front of them. The consideration of hypothetical situations like these is the essence of theoretical verification.

The logical positivists felt so strongly about the importance of verification that they refused to consider seriously any belief that is not *falsifiable*. They believed that if there is no possibility of disproving something, then it is not worth believing, because it is nothing more than mere speculation. Due to their strict adherence to this principle, the logical positivists rejected metaphysics altogether, including religious belief. If we do not wish to join them by making falsifiability an absolutely necessary criterion of belief, then we must determine how important it is to us. After all, many religious beliefs are not falsifiable.

For example, if someone claims to have been divinely healed of a malady, there is no way to determine the extent of divine intervention that may have taken place, if there was any at all. People are quick to believe that God has helped them. The question is whether we want to limit such claims in any way. Should I regard even the healing of a small scratch as a special divine act? Now consider a more controversial case. How do we respond when others claim that God has (mystically) spoken to them? It seems that such professions should be limited in some way, because it is highly unlikely that they are all legitimate. (There was an extended debate in eighteenth-century England over this matter. They referred to it as 'enthusiasm', a term coined by Locke to denote fanatical claims of personal religious inspiration.) On the other hand, dismissing all these claims out of hand may not be the best thing to do either. Essentially, there is no way to prove or disprove such beliefs.

The principle of falsifiability can be applied incrementally in two basic ways. In the first place, we can insist that certain *types* of beliefs be falsifiable. We might want to be optimistic about divine healing but sceptical about certain kinds of mystical experience. The principle of falsifiability can be applied according to a number of criteria regarding our beliefs, such as their potential harm or good, overall basis, etc. These factors may vary depending upon the circumstances, even for the same belief.

Second, we could require all beliefs to be falsifiable *to some extent*. This would involve assessing the probability of each belief, and this seems to be feasible as well. Even beliefs that cannot be proved or disproved can still be judged according to their likelihood. The credence we give a belief would correspond with its falsifiability. However, this is more than merely judging the probability of a belief being true. It is determining our *ability to judge its probability*, and this is therefore a more foundational type of assessment. In this way, falsifiability evaluates the *way* that we judge probability. A belief may seem highly probable from a given perspective, but if it is hardly falsifiable, then this suggests that the probability is being calculated on subjective bases. The more objective our beliefs are, the more falsifiable they will be. Consequently, the decision as to how much we will require our beliefs to be falsifiable boils down to the decision as to how objective we want our beliefs to be.

KNOWLEDGE

Many works on epistemology include some discussion about what constitutes knowledge. This sometimes begins with an analysis of the various nuances of the term 'know'. To be sure, we use this word in several ways, many of which are related to one another. These studies certainly have their own merit, but I believe that they miss the point slightly. The main thing that should concern us is how certain we can be about our beliefs. The act of holding beliefs with unshakeable certainty is what we generally refer to when we claim to have 'knowledge'. Indeed, knowledge can be regarded as belief that is certain and reliable. (We will examine the matter of certainty more closely a little later.)

However, knowledge is more than this, because we can be absolutely convinced of things that are incorrect. Consequently, it is generally accepted that something must be true before it can be regarded as knowledge. Once we add the criterion of truth to our definition of knowledge, it becomes apparent that the certainty we feel about what we regard as knowledge is essentially the certainty that these things are true. In other words, knowledge has a high level of certainty, and this certainty comes from being convinced of the truth of the matter.

Let us pause for a moment to consider an example. Suppose that Edna says she 'knows' that her family is going to throw her a surprise birthday party. She has reasons for believing this, but can her knowledge in this context be anything more than a belief of which she is very certain (of its truth)? If her birthday passes and the party does not take place, then we would conclude that she did not know about a party, because there was none. She was simply mistaken. This exposes the problem that underlies many claims to knowledge, namely the fact that our own fallibility makes it very difficult (if not impossible) to claim absolute certainty about our beliefs.

Some may challenge this conclusion by pointing out that the example is biased, because it only illustrates beliefs regarding future events, which obviously cannot be known with nearly as much certainty. This is a valid objection, so let us change the scenario. Let us now suppose that Edna says she knows that her family threw her a surprise party on her fortieth birthday. Unless there is reason to doubt Edna's sanity, we would not anticipate Edna being mistaken in this case. She was there and experienced the party first-hand, so we would not question her belief any further. It is a clear-cut belief based on personal experience that requires very little interpretation. Since it is more closely tied to simple empirical observation, it is more reliable.

What if we changed the nature of the belief itself? What would this do to Edna's claim to knowledge? Suppose Edna also says that she knows that her family did not give her that party out of love, but did it for some ulterior motive – for example, they wanted only to stay in her will and inherit her fortune. Edna may indeed have very compelling reasons for claiming this as well, but it should be obvious that she cannot have the same degree of certainty about this belief as she does about the party taking place. This belief requires broader inferences on her part. (This is what Peirce called 'abduction'.) It does not seem that Edna can know her family's motives to the same extent that she can know that the party actually occurred. Nevertheless, we do not want to say that she does not really know either of these things unless she can be absolutely sure of them. That would set the standard too high. We want knowledge to entail a high degree of certainty, but not absolute certainty.

There is still another aspect of this example which we have not yet considered. Let us assume that Edna is correct about both her beliefs. In the first situation, she is correct that a party will be held. In the second situation, she is correct about her family having ulterior motives. However, let us suppose that she does not have good reasons for either belief. In fact, we might say that she was just lucky in making the right call. Would we say that Edna *knew* these things? Probably not. There is indeed a difference between correct belief and knowledge. This is a distinction that goes all the way back to Plato. In effect, before I can claim to have knowledge of something, I must not only have a correct belief, but I must also understand *why it is correct*. I must understand the justification for the belief. Epistemologists thus commonly characterize knowledge as *justified, true belief*.

This brings us back full circle to the limits of knowledge. We are not infallible, and there is no completely objective perspective from which we can make judgements. However, we do not need to retreat into scepticism either. We can try to recognize our limitations and humbly seek the truth as best we can. If we really do esteem truth, we will want to embrace beliefs that are justifiable, and we will be modest in the claims we make. It does seem that there are some things of which we can be *very* sure (perhaps even absolutely sure) – things like empirical observations and strictly logical conclusions. However, these things comprise only a small portion of the beliefs we hold, since most of our beliefs require broader inferences. This is especially true of religious belief, which is highly speculative. After all, religions generally recognize these limitations, describing religious belief more aptly as *faith*.

EVIDENCE

There are no rules that dictate how much we should demand of belief. Some people demand a lot, others very little. There are three basic questions that we can ask, though, in making this determination. First, '*What counts as evidence?*' Empiricists argue that all our ideas are rooted in sensory experience, and they thus limit evidence to that which is empirically grounded. Others (e.g. rationalists and mystics) believe that there are other sources of knowledge, and they allow many other things to count as evidence. In contrast, sceptics allow very little, sometimes nothing at all. For them, all evidence and truth are strictly subjective.

Second, '*How much evidence should be required to support belief?*' The debate between Clifford and James in the late nineteenth century was over this precise issue. Clifford argued that it is unethical to believe something without sufficient evidence. James felt that we are justified in holding beliefs as long as they: 1) have some basis; 2) are useful; and 3) are not refuted by contrary evidence. We must indeed decide if we are entitled to belief or if we must be justified in believing something. Moreover, we must also wrestle with the matter regarding how much evidence is needed to compel us to accept or reject certain beliefs.

Third, '*How far can we go in making inferences?*' Peirce suggested that intellectual progress only occurs through abduction, i.e. the process of making inferences that are broader than strictly logical conclusions. The amount of liberty we take in making inferences critically affects the scope and the solidity of our beliefs. If we form beliefs very conservatively, our beliefs will be very solid but have limited relevance, since we are unwilling to extend them very far. In other words, if we wish to avoid jumping to false conclusions, we must limit the number of conclusions we make. On the other hand, if we form beliefs freely and liberally, we may indeed have a broader range of beliefs with a greater scope of relevance, but each of our beliefs will now be more susceptible to error, since we do not scrutinize them as closely. This is the trade-off that we must take into consideration.

Each of these three questions represents a point of tension in the formation of belief, and it seems unwise to try to relieve the tension in one direction or the other. Even the pursuit of truth must be tempered somewhat so that it does not fossilize into perfectionism or absolutism. As I indicated in the Introduction, it is tempting to avoid one extreme by gravitating to the opposite extreme. This is why it is commonly said that extreme begets extreme. When people encounter extremism, they must either embrace it or defend themselves against it. All too often, this results in creating more extremists, who either become like those who influenced them or react against the extremism so strongly that they become extremists of the opposite sort. Gravitating to the extremes is also tempting because it casts off the responsibility and effort required in maintaining the points of tension. It is simply easier to give up the fight. However, intellectual maturity requires us to maintain the points of tension. It requires us to truly aspire for ideals while recognizing our limitations in this pursuit. We must always seek the truth without making our claims on it too bold.

CHAPTER 8

SYSTEMATIZED BELIEF

As we have noted repeatedly throughout the book, we form beliefs in order to make sense of the world (and ourselves as well). All belief begins with sensory perceptions, and we relate them to one another in some way. Each belief we hold is thus a conglomerate of more basic beliefs. In general, belief is necessary for processing information. As more and more information is added to the pool, the task becomes increasingly difficult, so we attempt to simplify the process by constructing models and theories, more generally referred to as paradigms.

CONSTRUCTING PARADIGMS

The term 'paradigm' was used by philosopher of science Thomas Kuhn in his groundbreaking book *The Structure of Scientific Revolutions*, which first appeared in the 1960s. Kuhn contends that scientists typically construct paradigms (i.e. comprehensive models) to explain all observations that have taken place up to that point in time. Paradigms are working models that allow scientists to account for data and make predictions, and these predictions are then tested through experimentation. Paradigms integrate a number of more basic theories (e.g. equations and models) into a cohesive system. Some examples of paradigms are Newton's laws of motion, the economic systems of capitalism and communism, and the Christian doctrine of the Trinity.

Kuhn observes that many paradigms typically become outdated and are eventually replaced by newer ones. He refers to each of these replacements as a 'paradigm shift'. Each paradigm shift is preceded by a period of time when scientists try to modify the old paradigm in order to keep it useful. After the new paradigm is introduced, its acceptance is usually not immediate, because it must be proved to some extent before it can be trusted, particularly for making predictions. Besides, many people resist change and are reluctant to give up old paradigms, especially if they still 'work' for them. Consider how long it would take for a complete reform of the US social security system.

A paradigm shift also requires all information previously interpreted through the old paradigm to be reinterpreted according to the new one. In many scientific paradigm shifts where new paradigms are simply more accurate than old ones, this is a relatively light burden, because the old paradigms still have limited usefulness. For example, Einstein's theories did not make Newton's laws of motion irrelevant. However, whenever the paradigm shift entails a more fundamental change in thinking, it necessitates an intellectual 'revolution'. In such cases, old interpretations must be discarded before the new paradigm can be fully utilized. Moreover, other paradigms are also affected, since paradigms are typically interconnected. A paradigm shift of this magnitude thus results in the revision of a number of paradigms. For instance, our knowledge of mental illness has affected our thinking in several ways. We no longer try to cast demons out of epileptics and schizophrenics through exorcisms or by boring holes through their skulls, nor do we treat mental illness exclusively with counselling or with medication.

Good paradigms have a number of common characteristics. The more that paradigms possess these characteristics, the better they are. To start, good paradigms are *well founded*. They seek to interpret real data and are not based on mere speculation. Good paradigms are also *comprehensive*. They take into account all of the available data. They do not selectively choose the data which will be interpreted, but they try to make sense of all observations, including those which do not conform to general trends. Next, good paradigms are *coherent*. Paradigms must be logically consistent. They cannot interpret similar data in different ways or start with conflicting assumptions. Another thing that can be observed is that good paradigms are *progressive*. They are notable improvements over their predecessors. They must be able to encompass previous paradigms by accounting for all the data that has been interpreted up to that point in time.

In addition, a good paradigm is one that is *fruitful*, yielding reasonable predictions of new data. Good paradigms thus offer greater promise of intellectual advancement by extending the basis for both belief and speculation. Also, good paradigms are *efficient*. They produce good results for a modest investment. In other words, they are not too complicated or difficult to use. They do not necessarily need to be simple (because many things in life are not simple), but they should be straightforward. Their logic should be obvious. Last of all, good paradigms are *flexible*. They can easily be adapted and thus be useful for quite some time. Some of the most useful paradigms are those which have taken the longest time to replace, not because of their popularity, but because of their accuracy and flexibility.

ADAPTING PARADIGMS

All paradigms have a limited usefulness, since they are mere approximations of the true nature of things. Consequently, they eventually reach the limits of their productiveness, being unable to account for new data. Most often, this is determined by our limits of observation. As our observations become more precise, they begin to extend beyond the limits of our paradigms. However, sometimes we make anomalous observations, i.e. we see new things that do not fit our previous experience in general, and it becomes obvious that the paradigms we are using at the time are inadequate. In either case, as the limits of our paradigms are exceeded, exceptions are generated. In effect, paradigms are then considered to be valid *except* in particular circumstances.

Whenever a paradigm proves to be inadequate in some way, the first line of response is to adapt it. The adaptation must allow the paradigm to account for the exceptions which have been generated. As a result, every time the paradigm is adapted, its complexity is increased, and this makes it more difficult to use. After a while, the paradigm becomes impractical, making it obvious that a better paradigm is needed. For a number of years, scientists used Rutherford's 'plum pudding' model of the atom, and it became increasingly difficult to use this model, since it was inadequate in many respects. It was ultimately replaced by Bohr's model, which essentially eliminated the discrepancies by accounting for them within the theory itself. In evaluating paradigms, it is wise to apply a principle known as Ockham's Razor, named after William of Ockham, a notable philosopher of the scholastic period. Ockham suggested that it is always preferable to employ the simplest adequate explanation.

This is truly valuable advice. We should indeed be wary of convoluted explanations, because they are often nothing more than rationalizations that cannot be logically supported. People go far out of their way arguing points in order to avoid accepting things that are obvious and straightforward. Many sophisticated arguments thus tend to be counter-intuitive, and they reveal a desire to protect belief rather than pursue truth. This is not to say that the truth is always simple, because many things are truly complex and should not be oversimplified – this is the other extreme to be avoided. In *oversimplification*, people do not wish to pursue the truth, and so they find the simplest explanation which will be of some use to them or at least not cause them much harm. In *overcomplication*, people wish to avoid the truth by ignoring things that obviously contradict their beliefs, and they go to great lengths to ignore these contradictions through some kind of rationalization.

In both cases, the truth is sacrificed. However, those who overcomplicate matters are better able to mask their reluctance to embrace the truth, because they have some appearance of being objective. After all, it is easier to tell that something is being ignored when there is a lack of effort. When there is too much effort, the perpetrators can try to claim that others are actually missing something. For example, Thomas Aquinas constructed detailed arguments in order to argue that although the bread and wine of the Eucharist have the *form* (i.e. physical attributes) of bread and wine, they actually have the *substance* (i.e. spiritual being) of the body and blood of Christ. Hence, the wine and bread are really the body and blood of Christ, but we are unable to discern them as such. Of course, Protestants later rejected this doctrine, believing that the obvious was being overlooked – the elements are *really just* bread and wine. Many religious doctrines rely on this type of overcomplication, because they make metaphysical appeals that cannot be supported or refuted.

REPLACING PARADIGMS

As old paradigms become obsolete, there is increased pressure to replace them. After all, we still need to make sense of the world, and this necessitates having working paradigms. Besides, paradigms allow us to make progress by making it unnecessary to keep 'reinventing the wheel' and by providing contexts for new ways of thinking. These benefits are enhanced when old paradigms are replaced by others that are superior to them. In each instance, as a new paradigm emerges, dependence on the old paradigm is obviated, although there will still be those who obstinately cling to the old.

Constructing new paradigms involves creativity, because they must be more than modifications to old paradigms. New paradigms give us new ways of thinking, and these are birthed in the creativity of individuals and groups. Each attempt to construct a new paradigm involves an investment of time and energy, and each new paradigm must be validated before it can be fully trusted. Each candidate is analysed and tested, and if it passes scrutiny, it becomes the current working model until it is eventually replaced by another. Every useful paradigm consequently becomes a part of intellectual history. Paradigms from the past serve as reminders of the intellectual progress that has been made.

GROUP DYNAMICS

The process of creating and replacing paradigms is affected by group dynamics. We must be able to relate to others, and this compels us to use the same paradigms that are embraced by the group. Unless one is completely self-reliant and wishes to live as a recluse, this is a necessary part of life. We may still have differing opinions and views on an individual level, but we must be able to function within the predominant paradigms of society and of the groups to which we belong. Consequently, as more and more people are affected by paradigm shifts, the longer it takes for the shifts to occur, because more thinking and behaviour must be changed. Everyone may not see the need for change, and they may not want to alter their behaviour accordingly. Even those who do see a need for change may not understand the new paradigm, and this can impede progress as well. Too often, groups are reduced to the lowest common denominator (or slightly above it).

There are also trade-offs endemic to group dynamics that tend to slow down paradigm shifts. For example, group interests often clash with personal interests. What is best for the group is many times not best for each individual in the group. Such individuals will be reluctant to embrace the change, unless they decide to set aside their own interests in order to benefit the group. The larger the group, the less likely it is that everyone will be willing to do this. The most

THE MATURITY OF BELIEF

advantageous thing for the individual is to maximize the benefit received from being a part of the group while minimizing the cost of being a part of the group. In other words, groups tend to attract and reward 'takers', not 'givers'. There are very few groups in which the workload is distributed evenly.

Another trade-off that must be faced is that between short-term and long-term interests. Planning for the future most often requires a different course of action from living for the present. In groups of people, there will be disagreement over the emphasis that should be placed on both the present and the future. In fact, some people are short-sighted because they have difficulty evaluating long-term effects. A number of studies have shown that immediate interests often win out over long-term interests. This is why people tend to rationalize their participation in risky, destructive behaviour.

The organizational structure of groups likewise affects the way that paradigm shifts take place. In hierarchical structures, paradigm shifts are typically not permitted to threaten the hierarchy's power or authority. This is equally true of religious hierarchies, which commonly set themselves up as teaching authorities. A significant part of their power is due to influence, and this must be guarded most closely, since their authority is conversely based on their teaching. In effect, religious hierarchies claim to have God-given authority, and they justify their temporal authority by their claims to spiritual authority. In other words, they claim that their power is validated by the truth of their teaching. How do we know that their teaching is true? It is true because God put them in charge and thus guides them as they teach us. It is circular reasoning, pure and simple, and many of their constituents are blind to it.

Paradigm shifts cannot be forced upon the hierarchy. Rather, paradigm shifts are most often initiated by the hierarchy in order to reinforce its authority. Any time change takes place, the hierarchy must lead the way. Whenever possible, the hierarchy will control the paradigm shifts that take place, but when this is an impossibility, the hierarchy will appear to support the change even though it may be secretly opposed to it. In effect, hierarchies are often willing to make compromises in order to protect their power. Of course, hierarchies especially resist shifts in paradigms that directly undermine or threaten their power.

In situations where a hierarchical body exists within a democratic society, the hierarchy must appease the laity to some extent, because membership in the body is voluntary and cannot be forced. The democracy of the society at large empowers members of the group to the extent that they are free to leave the group at will. This relationship is illustrated in the spread of Catholicism to the United States. For centuries, the Roman Catholic Church had been dominant in Europe through the union of Church and state in the Holy Roman Empire. Although this power gradually eroded over time, there has historically been a difference between American and European Catholicism, largely due to the fact that democracy developed most quickly in the US. Even though the Roman Catholic Church maintains its hierarchical structure, it must appease its laity to some extent if it wants to have members who actively support the Church.

However, hierarchies in democratic societies can take steps to minimize the amount of control that must be yielded to the membership. (These steps are often taken in non-democratic societies as well.) First, the hierarchy can place heavy emphasis on indoctrination. This will help members to accept the authority of the hierarchy and recognize it as legitimate. Second, the hierarchy can advocate a sectarian view of other groups, casting aspersions on the various rivals of the hierarchy. Either of these first two ways can be solidified through 'orthodoxy', which we will discuss in the next chapter. Third, the hierarchy can solidify its power by increasing the dependency of its members. This dependency can be either religious or civil.

In democratic structures, change can take place more rapidly. However, some stability is sacrificed in the process. Greater freedom allows a greater range of opinions, and this produces a broader spectrum of change. Some changes are slight and gradual, while others are extensive and abrupt. Changes even take place in ways that are diametrically opposed to one another, and this often polarizes society. However, the benefits of being part of a larger society usually prevail over individual interests, and compromises are made in order to preserve the social order. Kant thus felt that economic considerations would continue to propel the world towards peace, even though small groups of people may try to oppose it. He also felt that religion too often hinders this progress instead of promoting it, and this is evidenced in the number of wars and disputes which have historically occurred in the name of religion.

Power is protected in democratic structures as well. The electorate do not want to lose their power, although they frequently surrender it by not exercising it. In democratic societies there is consequently a resistance to any kind of elite ruling class. Once again, this can be avoided only to a certain extent. The desire to retain control over one's own life includes limiting the influence of experts. The average person wants to be informed but does not want to feel compelled to blindly obey others. However, it can be argued that this happens routinely, since people are often influenced more than they realize. Even Jesus referred to the populace as 'sheep' in need of a 'shepherd'.

Democratic societies thus wish the intelligentsia to be at their service, not vice versa. This is why American colleges and universities are starting to displace trade schools. In order to compete for the money of the consumer, universities must be willing to teach what the people wish to learn. This has also resulted in a movement away from traditional, theoretical research towards more 'practical' types of research. Instead of broadening the theoretical base of knowledge, colleges and universities are instead sponsoring their faculties to complete community-oriented 'projects'. Professors likewise neglect critical, theoretical research and devote their energies to professionally related service projects, calling it 'scholarship'. Many schools are encouraging this. In a nutshell, democratic structures provide intellectual freedom, but economic concerns generally override other concerns, and much attention is devoted to catering to the whims of the consumer. This can actually hinder change, because it is difficult to replace paradigms that have gained popularity with the masses, especially when there is not sufficient respect for scholarship.

To be sure, there is greater stability in hierarchical structures. Progress is controlled, and this tends to keep things more focused and stable. In contrast, there is greater progress in democratic societies, because progress is allowed to run its own course; and since necessity is indeed often the mother of invention, progress will occur more rapidly when people are permitted (and required) to tend to their own needs. Nevertheless, this often takes place by trial and error, since there is generally a resistance to being controlled by experts. In hierarchical structures, expertise is not necessarily limited, but it is always controlled, because the intelligentsia itself must be controlled by the hierarchy. In both hierarchical and democratic organizations, knowledge is managed as a tool of the power base. In one case it serves the hierarchy, and in the other it serves the populace.

Perhaps the most significant difference between the two structures is in development. Without a doubt, the development of people is greater in democratic structures. As a rule, people mature by learning to think for themselves, and democracy gives them the freedom to do this. However, progress occurs in waves. It does not happen all of a sudden, because we all make mistakes, and this actually becomes one of our greatest sources of instruction. Hierarchies prevent many short-term failures and thus provide greater stability, but in so doing they preclude much long-term progress that could occur if more mistakes were allowed to be made. Of course, a society or organization cannot simply allow costly mistakes to be made, so some controls must be put in place. This is one area where expertise can be of help. There must be a healthy dependence upon expertise, especially as the knowledge base increases. Progress will be slow if we must constantly 'reinvent the wheel', so to speak. Informed individuals can rely on expertise without blindly following it, but this can only happen if people learn to think for themselves without becoming overly confident with their own opinions.

RELIGIOUS PARADIGMS

By their very nature, religious paradigms are extremely difficult to replace. As we have already observed, religious beliefs are highly speculative and cannot be proved or disproved. This protects them from being challenged, let alone replaced altogether. Since religious paradigms are essentially systems of belief, they share these same characteristics. We generally refer to the religious paradigms of religious organizations as doctrines. The high degree of subjectivity in religious belief accounts for the fact that there are countless numbers of religious doctrines being espoused in the world today. In spite of their subjectivity, religious doctrines can be criticized on the basis of their consistency. Religious groups consequently refine their doctrines in an attempt to make them coherent.

The thing that makes religious paradigms so precarious is their lack of empirical support. The key issue is: 'What is a sufficient basis for religious belief?' It is crucial to consider: 1) what will count as evidence; and 2) how much evidence will be required to support religious beliefs (and paradigms, doctrines, etc.). The problem with asking critical questions such as these is that we often cannot challenge the basis of particular doctrines without challenging the basis of religious belief altogether. For example, I cannot dispute the (Christian) charismatic doctrine of speaking in tongues without considering the authority and interpretation of Scripture, the relevance of personal experience and feelings, et al. If we argue that the doctrines of others are unfounded, we may have to face the fact that our own doctrines may not have any better foundation. Of course, there are some doctrines that do not have a solid basis at all. These can definitely be challenged, for they are little more than subjective feelings disguised as objective belief.

Another difficulty with religious paradigm shifts is the false authority that religious doctrines tend to assume. In effect, it is believed that since religious beliefs are sacred, they must trump everything else. As a result, religious doctrine too frequently grows into dogmatism. It took centuries for the Roman Catholic Church to admit its error in condemning Galileo, and it may likewise take centuries for fundamentalist Christians no longer to feel defensive about evolution. The tendency towards dogmatism is only complicated by group dynamics, since they affect religious paradigm shifts, too.

The subjectivity of religious belief has created (and continues to create) a vast array of religious doctrines and traditions in the world. Even within particular religious traditions, paradigm shifts are not accepted uniformly. Some groups replace paradigms, while others attempt to adapt them. The Protestant Reformation and the Catholic Counter-Reformation are good examples of this. Protestants rejected a number of Catholic doctrines, and even though the Catholics chose to retain those doctrines, they still found it necessary to revise them.

Progress can occur most freely when paradigms must compete with other paradigms. Intellectual monopolies do not engender progress, for they are only challenged whenever they fail internally. When we consider the subjectivity of religious belief, it becomes evident that religious monopolies can be sustained for long periods of time, because they are able to insulate themselves from competitors. This is especially true of religious organizations that are basically self-sufficient. Most religious traditions begin as reformation movements, but once they gain enough momentum and support to be self-sustaining, they tend to stagnate, because the emphasis shifts from growth to preservation. If there is to be maturity in religious belief, there must be an interaction of ideas. Religious paradigms must compete with other paradigms, both religious and non-religious. This requires an openness to truth and change, a vital part of intellectual maturity.

CHAPTER 9

SOURCES OF RELIGIOUS BELIEF

SUBJECTIVE AND OBJECTIVE SOURCES

We basically reason from two matrices of information. First, we rely on our own subjective/experiential matrix. This represents our own unique point of view, shaped by all the experiences we have had. Second, we also construct an objective/authoritative matrix. This includes things that we regard as objective or authoritative: parents, society and the laws of physics all fit into this category. In religious belief, this matrix includes things like Scripture and tradition. In general, things are objective or authoritative inasmuch as they lie or extend beyond our own personal perceptions and interests.

When we regard something as authoritative, this indicates that we have reasons to submit to it, and we thus allow it to override our personal perceptions and interests to that extent. Our reasons for doing this can be very broad or very narrow. For example, psychologist Lawrence Kohlberg observed that at the lowest level of moral development, children (and unfortunately some adults) are motivated primarily by reward and punishment. This is very selfish and narrow. However, if people mature and develop, they can be motivated for broader reasons, e.g. friendship, societal stability and justice. Carol Gilligan correctly pointed out a flaw in Kohlberg's theory, namely that morality is more than an appreciation for justice, which itself tends to be abstract. Morality also includes personal love, and yet we know that people can be loved either concretely or abstractly. We can also love either selfishly or unselfishly, so the dynamics are somewhat complex. In the final analysis, whether we submit to authority out of a sense of duty or out of love, our reasons can be either selfish or unselfish.

   Motivation affects the way we construct our objective/authorita-
tive matrix. We have incentives to count some things as objective or
authoritative, and we have incentives to exclude other things from
this matrix. Moreover, although we may have incentives to include
certain things, other opposing incentives may restrict our loyalty and
accountability to them. For example, I have incentives to trust my
physician, but I also have incentives to limit and qualify this trust.
In addition, the relationship between motivation and the objec-
tive/authoritative matrix can work in the other direction, too. Our
beliefs about what we regard to be objective or authoritative can
shape our motivations.
   For instance, let us suppose that Doris comes from a wealthy
family, and she regards the Bible as authoritative. Consequently,
when she reads verses like 'The love of money is the root of all evil'
and 'It is easier for a camel to go through the eye of a needle than
it is for a rich man to enter the kingdom of God,' her personal motivations interact with her objective/authoritative matrix. She feels a
need to live by these verses, and this affects her views on money and
wealth, hampering her motivation for prosperity. However, it is only
natural that she wants at least to maintain the lifestyle to which she
is accustomed, and this affects the way she interprets these verses
and the extent to which she will heed them. It is highly unlikely that
she will renounce all worldly goods, take a vow of poverty and join
a convent. She will probably moderate her lifestyle somewhat,
maintain some level of charitable giving, and do volunteer work,
perhaps.
   This is not to say that everyone who obeys authority does so with
honourable intentions. Many people appear to submit to external
authority, but they only do so for selfish reasons. They do not really
want to be objective or submissive. Rather, they conform to some
kind of standard because it benefits them in some way. Most often,
people have a desire to conform to the standards which are accepted
by others, since society generally rewards conformity and punishes
nonconformity. Conformity is primarily judged according to behaviour, due to the fact that we cannot really know the attitudes of
others. At best, we can only infer them from patterns of behaviour.
Too many parents are blind to this fact, and they are satisfied
with the mere behavioural conformity of their children. They do not
realize that obedient behaviour does not always come from an
obedient or cooperative spirit.

It is good to keep the subjective/experiential and objective/ authoritative matrices in tension with one another. Unfortunately, some people operate primarily (perhaps exclusively) from one matrix or the other, and this leads to excesses. There are those whose self-esteem is so low that they disregard their own perceptions and feelings. Their thinking is by and large determined externally. They are influenced rather easily, and they are extremely docile. In contrast, there are others who have little or no regard for anything or anyone beyond themselves. All their thinking and behaviour is determined internally from a selfish, subjective point of view. They may try to mask their selfishness, or they may be openly selfish and belligerent.

As a general rule, we interpret each matrix within itself and with respect to the other matrix. In other words, our personal experiences are interpreted by previous personal experiences that we have had. Likewise, we judge objective and authoritative sources by one another. Each source of authority is scrutinized according to other sources of authority. Also, it is normal and healthy for our subjective and objective perspectives to interact, and we have already noted an example of this.

We do not have any difficulty forming a subjective perspective. This is what comes most naturally to us. The problem we encounter is in forming an objective perspective. Since we cannot perceive things from an entirely objective point of view, and since we cannot be motivated without some self-interest, we must relate to the objective with some subjectivity. Consequently, we should strive to be as objective as possible. This does not mean minimizing or ignoring the subjective point of view. Rather, it involves broadening and deepening our overall perspective so that the subjective can be better understood within a broader context. In other words, I should recognize my own point of view and grasp how it relates to the perspectives of other people. The more I understand other perspectives, the better I can see myself within the bigger picture.

THE FOUR SOURCES

There are typically four epistemological sources that inform religious belief: Scripture, tradition, reason and experience. They are often prioritized in that order by Protestants, because this helps to minimize religious subjectivity. Nevertheless, I prefer to discuss them in the reverse order, since this more accurately reflects how these sources are formed.

First, *experience* is the basic building block of all knowledge. Everything that we believe is grounded in some type of experience. As such, experience provides the content of the other three sources. Even Scripture is based upon experience. Ancient people had particular experiences which inspired the writing of the texts. They claimed to have witnessed special events, both natural and supernatural. They also made claims of mystically receiving supernatural revelation from God. These experiences are thus the foundation of Scripture. Likewise, experience is more broadly the foundation of all belief.

However, experience as mere phenomena has no meaning. Experience must be interpreted. This was discussed at the beginning of Chapter 1. A situation was posed in which you are walking down an alley late at night and suddenly feel something poking you in the back. You might interpret this experience as potentially threatening, but if you should recognize a familiar voice behind you, your interpretation would most likely be very different. All in all, experience itself provides the raw data for all belief and knowledge, but experience must be interpreted before it can have any meaning.

As a result, it is necessary for *reason* to process experience and make sense of it. Reason is accordingly regarded as the second source of religious belief. In reality, it is a mistake to consider experience and reason as distinct sources of religious belief, because they are fundamental to all belief. Experience and reason cannot be disconnected from tradition and Scripture, and they cannot be separated from one another. Experience is meaningless unless it is interpreted by reason, and reason is dependent upon experience to provide it with information to process. Even purely theoretical concepts are abstracted from experience. However, experience and reason are still separate sources of religious belief in the sense that they extend beyond the confines of tradition and Scripture.

It is likewise faulty to claim that tradition and Scripture cannot or should not be judged by reason. Indeed, they are formed by reason as well. Of course, someone might contend that Scripture was inspired in such a way as to bypass the reasoning of the biblical authors; they simply wrote down words. (This is known as the dictation theory of inspiration.) Accepting this leads to the conclusion that Scripture was produced through divine reason alone, independent of human reasoning. This is untenable on several accounts. In the first place, the text would have to be inerrant in every respect, and given the discrepancies and inaccuracies of the various texts we have, this is simply not feasible. However, even if we could not find any discrepancies or inaccuracies in the texts, on what basis could we reasonably believe that none could ever be found for all time and eternity?

Let us pretend for a moment that Einstein's theories are so airtight that we cannot find any flaws in them. Could we safely assume that nobody will ever find any flaws in them? If Einstein claimed that he received his theories directly from God, would that convince us? I would hope that we would not be so naive. In effect, even if it were true that Scripture was inspired apart from human reasoning, we would not be able to discern such through our reasoning either. This would also have to be mystically revealed to us by God. I have actually heard people argue this, and I am reminded of scores of Latter Day Saints who believe in the divine inspiration of the Book of Mormon based on a 'burning in the bosom' that they claim to experience. This illustrates the fact that since untenable claims cannot be supported rationally, they must be defended through naiveté and subjectivism.

Sad to say, those who embrace such a high mysticism (i.e. a belief that God is revealed and known apart from human reasoning) are often aloof to its implications. If God is known directly, then it does not seem that Scripture would be necessary at all. After all, God could just reveal truth to us – directly, mystically and personally. Furthermore, the only way to protect revelation from human foibles and limitations is to keep it out of human control altogether. God would need to be fully in control of the entire process, and this would lead to a strong form of determinism that many would not wish to embrace. We would be forced to conclude that God is simply revealed in varying degrees to different people. God enlightens some and keeps others in partial or total darkness. This is the kind of religious belief that still engenders prejudice and hostility around the world today.

All in all, the conclusion that must be reached is that *God is not revealed apart from human reason.* The texts of Scripture were written through the reasoning of the authors as they reflected upon the experiences they had. Their faculties and their understanding were not bypassed. Rather, the texts reflect their individual perspectives, and this includes their limitations as well. Religions teach that their sacred texts are divinely inspired. I have not tried to debunk this belief in any way, but I have tried to show that it is unreasonable to have a view of divine inspiration that is so high that human abilities are bypassed in the process. It must be conceded that whether or not particular texts are divinely inspired, they are still human products. This is more consistent with other commonly held religious beliefs. For example, many believe that God speaks to them through others (e.g. clergy, family, friends), but they do not necessarily regard these people as inerrant. We can similarly believe that God speaks to us individually, but this does not require us to consider ourselves inerrant either.

Not only are tradition and Scripture formed by reason, but they are scrutinized by it as well. In fact, everything is judged by reason. The key is the criteria by which things are judged. Whether one accepts or rejects the authority of particular religious traditions or texts, a judgement is being made nonetheless. If we really do see the value of striving for objectivity in our beliefs, then we should not naively accept claims of authority and/or inerrancy. Some type of objective criteria must be applied.

As the third source of religious belief, *tradition* represents collective reasoning regarding shared experience. Groups of people share the same beliefs, and the basis of this is some kind of common experience. As traditions grow and include more people, they tend to become splintered. Experience becomes more diverse within the group, and this makes it more difficult for people to relate to one another and share beliefs in common. Moreover, the sheer increase in numbers makes it more likely that opinions will differ, even when experiences are still shared.

Even diverse traditions can achieve and maintain some level of unity. People can rally around common goals or values, joining together through a unified vision of the world. People can also come together under the umbrella of authority, which we will consider shortly. Authority can be given to the group itself, and this can be controlled democratically or delegated from one individual to another. However, the dynamics are different when authority is given to tradition itself (as opposed to the group). This essentially makes the group beholden to the past in some way, and this limits change by requiring it to be legitimated by the beliefs that need to be replaced.

For instance, in Catholicism many papal encyclicals try to legitimate proposed changes by showing how the changes are consistent with earlier Catholic teachings. Protestant groups that give authority to tradition likewise feel a need to legitimate change by connecting it with the past. Quite often, key figures like Luther, Calvin and Wesley are cited. Granting authority to tradition limits change and, as we have already noted, limiting change stifles progress but provides stability. This is the trade-off, so the more authority that tradition is given, the more that stability is given precedence over progress.

The fourth source of religious belief is *Scripture*. Religions like Judaism, Christianity and Islam are known as 'revealed' faiths, because they believe that divine truth has been supernaturally revealed to them. In these religions, particular texts are regarded as being divinely inspired, and this is what separates them from other texts. Scripture is thus deemed to be a form of *special revelation*, i.e. a means through which God is specially revealed. This distinguishes it from *natural revelation*, which is God's self-revelation in the world (through nature and natural means). The other special revelation that Christians recognize is the incarnation. This is the doctrine that God became a human being, namely Jesus Christ. He was fully God and fully man, and he thus reveals God to us in a special way.

However, there is growing support for pluralism today. According to pluralism, God is revealed in many different ways. No single religion has exclusive claims to the truth, but all religions reveal God to some extent. Christian pluralism is indeed interesting to observe, because Jesus made several exclusive claims that cannot be so easily ignored. For example, in the Gospel of John, Jesus claims to be the way to eternal life and to God, and this has traditionally been understood as an exclusive claim. A number of pluralists typically reinterpret these passages in some way. Moreover, since pluralism by definition rejects all exclusive claims, it is not uncommon for Christian pluralists to hold a lower view of Scripture and at least question the divinity of Jesus.

As I mentioned in the Introduction, I do not find pluralism to be very convincing, because it just seems unreasonable to conclude that if God wants to be revealed in the world, the best way to accomplish this is for God to be revealed in different (and often contradictory) ways to different groups of people. It would appear that one general type of revelation might be more effective. Nevertheless, evolution has greatly complicated this possibility. Of course, one could either deny special revelation altogether or just regard one revealed faith as the true faith, excluding all other claims of revelation. The latter can be rationalized if one concludes that God is not interested in the salvation of all, but only in the salvation of a select few. However, this is the kind of dangerous religious teaching that continues to threaten peace and stability in the world. In consideration of how speculative and subjective our religious beliefs are, I do not feel that there is any way to justify embracing such a view with any significant level of certainty, since it is so destructive.

On the other hand, if special revelation is regarded as exclusive, it is difficult to reconcile that with the belief that God loves all people equally and desires the salvation of everyone. Kant correctly observed that a revealed faith cannot be a universal faith, because everyone cannot have equal access to it. Even among those who have equal exposure to a particular teaching, some are more inclined to believe than others, based on their personalities, past experiences, etc. This is why a number of Christians are questioning the traditionally held notion of hell (where unbelievers are punished eternally without any future hope of salvation) and are instead leaning towards some type of pluralism or universalism. Another option is to regard salvation as being already extended to humanity as a whole, but then individuals can forfeit this through their own rebellion. John Wesley's doctrine of prevenient grace was constructed along these lines.

To summarize, if one wishes to believe in special revelation, then much caution must be taken as the implications are worked out. Since religious belief is by nature very tentative, I am convinced that we cannot justify people boldly championing the belief that God only loves a select group of people, since that contains many seeds of destruction and hatred. Viewing God as strict and demanding is not just dangerous, it essentially portrays God as being rather incompetent, since it does not appear that God has been very successful in being unequivocally revealed to humanity. On the other hand, the belief that God loves everyone equally is difficult to reconcile with a belief in special revelation, especially the traditional doctrine of hell, because everyone does not have equal access to that revelation or equal ability to understand it. In the end, whether one accepts or rejects the notion of special revelation, God needs to be seen as rather tolerant and patient, perhaps more interested in our growth and maturity than in a simple obedience that condones and perpetuates intellectual immaturity.

RELIGIOUS AUTHORITY

Whenever unity and continuity are desired, subjectivism must be controlled. One way to do this is for everyone to *strive to be objective*, and I would argue that this is the best way to foster maturity. However, subjectivism is often controlled through the exercise of *authority*. Since the thing that is really controlled is people, the authority that is exercised must be legitimate and it must be kept in check. Authority is certainly valid when people freely choose to accept it or be part of a group or society that employs it. Nevertheless, this merely gives authority a subjective legitimacy, because it only asserts that people have the right to be governed if they so choose. Our interest is in exploring the possible objective bases for religious authority in matters of belief. In other words, we need to consider the extent to which we should be accountable to external sources in forming our religious beliefs. The two obvious sources of religious authority to examine are Scripture and tradition, and I will conclude with some brief remarks about orthodoxy.

Scripture

The authority of Scripture is most often founded upon belief in its inspiration. After all, if it is divinely inspired, then it has direct authority over all people, speaking to us as the instrument of God. However, although divine inspiration can be inferred, it cannot be established. There is no way to empirically determine to what extent a person may be divinely influenced, if at all. Consequently, it is wholly a matter of faith to assert that particular texts are inspired by God, and yet religious devotees do so with great conviction.

From ancient times to the present, there have consistently been a few bases on which people have commonly affirmed the divine inspiration of individuals and the texts that they author. The first of these is *miracles*. Since people generally regard miracles as divine acts, miracle-workers are looked on as divinely gifted individuals, and their utterances are respected as prophetic. According to this belief, miracles identify those who have been specially selected to be divine mouthpieces. Although this was widely accepted in ancient cultures, support for it has waned over the centuries. To start, the reality of miracles in general has been challenged by scientists and philosophers. Moreover, even among those who do believe in them, many no longer regard them as necessarily communicating any divine message or pointing out the 'prophets' among us. However, it is surprising how many people are still influenced in this way.

Another way that 'prophets' have been 'identified' throughout history is by their *ability to foretell the future*. Since only God knows the future, the apparent ability to predict future events is understood as a divine gift. Once again, these claims have also been debunked throughout the centuries. In the first place, these 'prophetic' passages almost always use symbolic language, and this makes their meaning obscure and rather fluid. A particular passage can be interpreted in a number of ways. This is true of both religious and non-religious writings, e.g. the 'prophecies' of Nostradamus and horoscopes. With respect to the prophetic passages in Scripture, scholars question the date of authorship of many of these passages. Based on the analysis of scriptural texts, including comparisons between them and other ancient texts, it seems likely that many scriptural prophecies may not have been written as early as they claim to be.

The bottom line is that it is very risky to base the authority of Scripture on the reality of supernatural 'signs' like miracles and prophecies. Furthermore, the authority of Scripture cannot be established through appeals to *circular arguments*. For example, when asked why they believe that the Bible is divinely inspired, a number of Christians will respond 'Because 2 Timothy 3.16 says so.' A number of religious texts claim to be divinely inspired, but simply making the claim does not make it true. If I were to conclude this book with 'Every word in this book was inspired by God,' that would prove nothing. In fact, if there were no other reason to believe my claim, my willingness to make it would actually make me seem less credible, because that would indicate that I am either deceptive or misguided. In the same way, rejecting the claims of 'prophets' does not necessarily make them either liars or lunatics, as C. S. Lewis suggested about Jesus (*Mere Christianity*, New York: Macmillan, 1943, 54–6). They might simply be well-meaning, misguided souls.

Another circular argument that is often used is an appeal to the reliability of the Church (or the tradition more generally). It is argued that Scripture is divinely inspired (and inerrant) because the Church is divinely inspired (and inerrant), and vice versa. In other words, we can trust Scripture because it is sanctioned by the Church. Why should we trust the Church? Because the Church is guided by the Holy Spirit. How do we know this? Because Scripture tells us so. The argument goes round and round in a circle, trying to base the authority of Scripture on the authority of the Church, while simultaneously resting the authority of the Church on the authority of Scripture. Each side of the argument supports the other, so the argument is certainly coherent. However, since the authority of Scripture ultimately rests on itself, the argument begs the question (i.e. assumes the conclusion from the beginning).

In a similar fashion, claims of scriptural inerrancy cannot be supported rationally. There are too many internal inconsistencies within the texts themselves. Passages simply disagree with one another. For example, nobody can objectively deny that the biblical books of Romans and James give contrasting views on the role of good works in the Christian life. Romans declares that we are justified through faith alone, but James says that works are necessary for salvation, because works are the evidence of faith. Martin Luther recognized this. Since he was firmly committed to 'justification by faith alone', he did not support the inclusion of the book of James in the canon, but others disagreed and the book James remained in the Protestant Bible. Adherents of scriptural inerrancy go to great lengths to try to reconcile or trivialize such internal contradictions in the text, but these efforts are futile; the inconsistencies remain there nonetheless. In fact, it can be argued that the canon of Scripture intentionally includes opposing viewpoints that must be kept in tension.

In addition to the internal inconsistencies, there are numerous historical and scientific discrepancies in the scriptural texts. For instance, some scholars have questioned whether the city of Jericho actually existed at the time that the Israelites supposedly conquered it under the leadership of Joshua. Many similar examples could be cited. With all of these difficulties, the supposed inerrancy of Scripture is by no means self-evident. As a result, a belief in the inerrancy of Scripture is ultimately a belief in the inerrancy of canonization, because tradition itself has produced the canon of Scripture by deciding what texts should be regarded as authoritative. Whatever authority one ascribes to Scripture must also be ascribed to those who selected the texts to be included in the canon, and this makes inerrancy even more untenable. Many fundamentalists fail to recognize this.

If all this is true, then what are the possible bases for scriptural authority? There are essentially three options for establishing the authority of Scripture. First, it can be based on the *reliability of tradition*, since it is tradition itself that asserted this authority in the first place. Past generations believed that particular texts should be regarded as authoritative, and this becomes a basis for accepting this authority today. If we are not asserting the inerrancy of Scripture, then it is not necessary to assert that the tradition is inerrant. Rather, we can affirm the authority of Scripture to the extent that we can trust the tradition itself. Indeed, many Christians feel that the willingness of the early Christians to be martyred for their faith confirms their sincerity, and this helps to validate the things that they claimed and believed. However, sincerity alone is not enough to validate a belief, so trust in tradition must be more than this. Moreover, it must be kept in mind that the intellectual standards of past generations are not nearly the same as those we employ today. The mere fact that people many years ago believed something does not necessarily compel us to believe it today. Our trust in tradition must thus be qualified by evaluating the credibility of our forebears.

Second, some try to base the authority of Scripture on its *historical veracity*. Various theologians have contended that the literal, historical resurrection of Christ is essential to Christian faith. As such, the resurrection substantiates the divinity of Christ and essentially vindicates the New Testament account of him and his followers. The problem with this is that the resurrection of Christ can be neither confirmed nor refuted. The testimony of Scripture (primarily the Gospels) is the basis that Christians have for believing in the resurrection. The matter ultimately rests on the reliability of tradition, since it cannot otherwise be corroborated.

Affirming the historicity of the Old Testament narratives is even more problematic, because there are a number of discrepancies, both within the texts themselves and with other historical and scientific sources. All in all, it is rather precarious to base the authority of Scripture on its historical accuracy, and I believe that very few Christians actually do so. Rather, Christians who insist on the historical accuracy of the texts typically make this assertion based on their belief in the inerrancy of Scripture. They start with a belief in the divine inspiration of Scripture; this leads them to accept its inerrancy; and they subsequently conclude that the narratives must be accurate. They reason in this manner due to the fact that the authority of Scripture cannot be established by the historical veracity of the texts. The greatest possible exception to this is the accuracy of the Gospels, especially the resurrection accounts. However, as I have already indicated, the veracity of these accounts ultimately rests on the reliability of tradition.

Third, the authority of Scripture can be based on the *relevance of its message*, both its relevance to us personally and its universal relevance to all of humanity. This is essentially the line of reasoning advanced by Kant. He scoffed religious tradition, and he felt that the historical veracity of Scripture cannot be confirmed. Nevertheless, he asserted the authority of the Bible, primarily because he respected its moral teachings, especially the teachings of Christ, which he claimed were morally superior to anything that had been written up to that point in time, including the moral philosophy of the ancient Greeks (Plato, Aristotle, et. al.). This interpretation of Christianity became the basis for much of the liberal Protestant theology that emerged throughout the nineteenth century, and it still wields considerable influence today. Although all Christians would affirm the relevance of the message of Scripture, many would reject the notion that this is the primary, if not the sole, basis of scriptural authority, since this does not require Scripture to be historically or otherwise inerrant. In fact, this view permits Scripture to be regarded allegorically like Aesop's fables, for instance.

Even though the authority of Scripture is frequently based on one or more of these three things, none of them can authenticate divine inspiration. Unless one considers tradition to be inerrant, the imprimatur of tradition does not necessarily indicate that a document is divinely inspired. Historical accuracy will not establish inerrancy either. There are many documents that are historically accurate, but they are not divinely inspired. Similarly, there are many texts that are relevant to us and to others, but there is no reason to necessarily regard them as divinely inspired either. Aristotle and Einstein are both relevant, but that does not mean that God spoke through them. Nevertheless, these three things still remain the possible bases of scriptural authority. In consideration of the difficulties encountered in trying to establish historical accuracy, we must reject it as a trustworthy basics. This narrows our options to the reliability of tradition and the relevance of the message, and these represent the bases that Christians have commonly relied on in asserting the authority of Scripture.

What is needed is a mediated position regarding scriptural authority. The doctrine of *accommodation* is helpful in formulating such a position. This teaches that God is revealed to us at our own levels of understanding. It is thus unnecessary to regard scriptural texts as inerrant. Rather, the texts reflect the understanding of the authors.

We can learn from them, but we can also move beyond their limitations because *revelation is progressive*. Although God may have been revealed more intimately at certain points in history, God is gradually revealed over time. In this way, our understanding of God builds on the understanding of past generations, including the authors of scriptural texts. Scripture itself is a resource that does not need to be interpreted and applied literally.

It is also helpful to affirm the *complementarity of special and general revelation*. In other words, a belief that God is revealed specially through Scripture does not preclude one from believing that God is more generally revealed in the world itself. Moreover, these two types of revelation are complementary. Of course, it is much easier to assert this once the false expectation of inerrancy is surrendered. This allows Scripture and other sources of knowledge to inform one another and to be integrated into a cohesive whole. Religion can thus be reconciled with history, science, philosophy, etc. Along the same lines, Scripture itself must be understood in light of *critical scholarship*. The texts were written in specific contexts, and they were often motivated by personal and provincial agendas – religious, political, moral, etc. Critical scholarship can help us to understand how and why the texts were written, and this can enlighten the way we apply them to our own situations and contexts.

Last of all, we must recognize that *the authority of the scriptural canon rests on the authority of tradition*. Some religions are based upon one central text, but others like Christianity are more broadly based on a religious tradition. Consequently, the Christian tradition has produced numerous texts, and since the texts vary in many ways, Christians have had to decide how much authority each text should carry. Christianity has thus selected particular texts to be part of the canon of Scripture, and this is what we come to know as the Bible. God did not send down a list from heaven to identify the texts that should be regarded as authoritative. Instead, the Christian tradition itself has decided what texts should have authority. Other texts have been either ignored or condemned. All in all, the scriptural canon derives its authority from tradition, since that is its point of origin.

Tradition

In discussing the authority of religious tradition, it is not necessary to discuss the legitimacy of following tradition in general. People certainly have the right to adhere to tradition if they so choose, and this can be either a personal choice or the choice of the group. Instead, our concern is the extent to which our beliefs should be accountable to tradition in the interest of objectivity. Within Christianity, tradition is not given uniform attention. Some groups believe that authority must be delegated, and the best example of this is Catholicism, which not only teaches that authority is delegated from Christ to the Church, but also asserts that the Church is inerrant in its teachings. This places undue stress on tradition, giving it a prominence that is incidentally unjustified, one that essentially makes people slaves to the past. New ideas must somehow be shown to be consistent with old ones. It cannot simply be concluded that old ideas are just wrong or inadequate. It is hard to tell how long Catholic thinkers will have to continue wrestling with Augustine and Aquinas. To a great extent, Catholic thought is still stuck in the medieval period, and individual Catholics cannot ignore this era, even if they want to.

In contrast with this position is the view that authority should be determined democratically. The group decides how it will be governed, and this allows the group to determine what role tradition will play, if any. As postmodernism has unfolded, the stress on tradition has steadily declined, and the change has been significant. Indeed, many groups give no place to tradition at all and simply 'do their own thing', so to speak. This is rather unfortunate, because tradition can play a very positive role in guiding beliefs, particularly in groups. Tradition brings *unity* to the group as it centres the focus of its members around an already established core of beliefs. This gives the group a certain *consistency*, which in turn enhances the group's long-term *stability*. Also, tradition often provides us with *lessons from the past*, and this can inform our beliefs.

Notwithstanding these benefits, tradition can also have a negative impact. It is often used as a means to *control* others. A minority insists that the majority conform to the beliefs of past generations, and they are able to convince the majority to do this by bestowing upon tradition an air of sacredness. Tradition carries such weight that there must be overwhelming reasons to justify a departure from it. Although this may initially prevent some difficulties, it eventually produces *stagnation* in the long run. Growth and development are prevented, and this essentially thwarts the maturity of group members. Since beliefs are largely (if not entirely) dictated by the past, members end up living in a state of *dependency*, being unable and/or unwilling to think for themselves.

This is precisely what Kant condemns in his essay 'What Is Enlightenment?' He concludes that people predominantly live under self-incurred tutelage. They gladly remain immature due to laziness and cowardice. The public grants authority to guardians, who generally keep it unenlightened. Many of the guardians themselves are incapable of enlightenment, and they persuade the public to restrict the few enlightened guardians who actually try to enlighten the masses. Kant believes that dogma and creeds are a misuse of our natural endowments and are the 'ball and chain' of permanent immaturity. This is particularly true of religious dogma, because religious incompetence is the most harmful and degrading form of incompetence. The way to find release from this bondage is through enlightenment. Kant urges us to have courage to think for ourselves. That is the motto of enlightenment.

According to Kant, it is more common for enlightenment to be hindered in public, rather than in private, because that is where it is a threat to the guardians. This is why we must be able to question conventions without inciting anarchy. One generation cannot put the next generation in a position where it would be impossible for it to extend and correct its knowledge or to make any intellectual progress. This would be a crime against humanity, whose destiny lies precisely in such progress. Kant feels that people will of their own accord gradually work their way out of barbarism so long as artificial measures are not deliberately adopted to keep them in it. As a result, the public use of human reason must always be free. It alone can bring about enlightenment. Civil freedom is what allows the intellectual freedom that is needed. However, the ruling body must be sufficiently enlightened so as to not be threatened by intellectual freedom, but capable of managing it.

When we weigh the advantages and disadvantages of following tradition, it becomes obvious that although tradition is a valuable resource, it cannot become the standard by which all things are judged. On the one hand, it is foolish to ignore tradition, since there is much that we can learn from it. On the other hand, tradition should not be used to stifle progress, development and maturity. Since there is no rational reason to regard people or organizations (even the Church) as inerrant, it is likewise foolish to regard tradition as sacred, something that always trumps other sources of information.

Orthodoxy

Tradition is frequently used to control people through the enforcement of orthodoxy. People are rejected or shunned if they do not hold the 'correct' beliefs; and orthodoxy itself generally requires some kind of coercion before it can be attained. When people are at liberty to think freely about religion, there is seldom much unity regarding doctrine. This is not surprising, because religion itself is largely non-empirical, and this requires it to be highly speculative. I have asserted this throughout the book, and history has repeatedly attested to this fact.

Consequently, orthodoxy is contextual. It is determined by a particular group within a particular context. Even specific Christian traditions vary in their beliefs in different cultural and historical settings. Granted, there are some doctrines that have been more or less accepted throughout Christian history, expressed in its ecumenical creeds. Nevertheless, these doctrines are rather basic, and there has never been a consensus about them. Many of these doctrines were decided at councils, and the results were at times forced through political power. Dissension always remained, but it was controlled for a while within the hierarchical Roman Catholic Church. However, first the Orthodox Churches broke away, then once the Protestant Reformation had taken root, Christianity became so splintered that it is now virtually impossible to speak of 'Christian orthodoxy' without qualifying the term contextually.

As a tool of tradition, orthodoxy can be employed either positively or negatively. On the positive side, it does *unite people through common belief*, giving them a common base. It thus helps to *maintain integrity* within particular traditions. On the negative side, orthodoxy ends up *dividing people from one another*. Dissenters are not accepted within the group. In fact, orthodoxy is many times used to *condemn others* who do not share a set of particular beliefs. The desire to enforce orthodoxy in this way can stem from fear. People may not want to face the fragility of their beliefs by having them questioned, or they may not want to change. Orthodoxy thus becomes a convenient way to *maintain the status quo*.

In thinking about orthodoxy, it is wise to keep in mind a distinction that is ultimately attributed to Augustine. He said that in essential things we should strive to have unity, but in non-essential matters there should be liberty to disagree; however, in all things a spirit of charity must prevail. If we would keep this in mind, we might see that many religious divisions are unnecessary, but are too often fuelled by little more than prejudice and self-centredness.

SECTION FOUR

MATURE BELIEF

CHAPTER 10

RELIGIOUS BELIEF AND CERTAINTY

THE DESIRE FOR CERTAINTY

It seems only natural to want to be certain of our beliefs, at least those that are important to us. As we have already observed, beliefs can be individually important to us for any number of reasons, both objective and subjective. They are also important to the extent that they are central to our entire belief system. In general, the more important specific beliefs are to us, the more important it is that we be certain of them. Religious beliefs are certainly significant to us, since they reflect the views that we have regarding the ultimate nature of the world, ourselves and reality. Also, religious beliefs are many times tied rather closely to self-image, affecting both the way we relate to others and our general outlook on life. For these reasons and others, religious beliefs are often a crucial part of our belief structure, and so we generally want to be more certain about them. We at least want to feel that there is not sufficient reason to doubt them.

Due to its metaphysical character, religious belief is somewhat dependent upon feelings of certainty, but this dependence is not always apparent. Since it can be neither proved nor disproved empirically, it is quite impervious to attack on objective grounds. For example, if belief in the existence of God cannot be demonstrated empirically, then it cannot be refuted empirically either. This kind of insulation can give us feelings of certainty about our religious beliefs, but these feelings are not all that stable, because they lack a strong objective basis. As is the case with subjective belief in general, religious belief is safe from attack due to the fact that there is not much of an objective basis to attack. As long as the beliefs are structured together in a coherent fashion, they are fairly safe. Of course, the more that religion attempts to make empirical claims, the more vulnerable it becomes. For example, it is much safer to assert who will go to heaven and who will go to hell than it is to claim that the earth was created in seven days. Only the second claim can be empirically tested.

To the extent that the certainty of religious belief cannot be derived from objective sources, it must rest on a more subjective basis. Consequently, although religious belief is relatively secure in one respect, it is still quite fragile. On the one hand, it is secure in the sense that it cannot be empirically refuted. On the other hand, it is fragile in the sense that there is a lack of compelling (i.e. objective) reasons to support it. Once religious belief moves away from foundationalism (in which certain foundations are accepted without question), it becomes increasingly subjective. As such, people do not feel compelled to accept the religious beliefs of others. Moreover, the lack of empirical corroboration can cause people to doubt their own religious beliefs, and many people are extremely uncomfortable if their beliefs are seriously questioned by others.

Religious beliefs thus need to be reinforced often if they are to be embraced enthusiastically. Individuals buttress their beliefs by engaging in particular practices (e.g. prayer, meditation and reading Scripture) that give them feelings of certainty and reassurance. At the corporate level, some religious traditions require their members to complete catechetical training in order to ensure thorough indoctrination. For other traditions, the reinforcement of religious beliefs entails a steady diet of teaching and/or preaching, and this can take place several times a week in some places. In Christian circles, some groups even find a weekly routine like this to be inadequate, and so special services, seminars, etc. are held periodically to rejuvenate their members. In all fairness, the need for reinforcement is not all due to the fragility of religious belief. Human nature itself is such that people must often have their enthusiasm rekindled, no matter what the group or the cause may be.

Nevertheless, the reinforcement of religious beliefs is clearly aimed at helping people to feel certain about their group's doctrine, and this is why it is usually supported by polemical apologetics. In other words, members are given plenty of reasons to embrace the doctrines, but counter-evidence is seldom considered. Instead, members acquire a false sense of certainty as their beliefs are continually reinforced, and they often develop a dependency on this reinforcement. As I have heard it stated, 'You will die spiritually if your soul doesn't get fed.' This is basically an admission that people realize deep down just how fragile many of their religious beliefs really are, and much of this fragility can be attributed to the absence of a strong objective basis for their beliefs.

Indeed, doubt itself is by and large condemned and regarded as a lack of faith. Certainty cannot be threatened, so planting seeds of doubt in the minds of others is strictly forbidden, even if this means merely pointing out the fallibility of our beliefs. The greater the number of beliefs that must be defended and the greater the subjectivity of these beliefs, the more that the group has to fear, usually evidenced by an increase in defensiveness. This can be observed in local churches and in religious educational institutions, which vary in their openness to questioning and exploring beliefs and ideas. One of the most telling signs is the group's attitude towards philosophy, which is a discipline devoted to raising questions, rather than dictating answers. In fact, some religious groups use philosophy only as a tool for apologetics and rhetoric. They do not study it for its own sake as an open-ended intellectual venture. Instead, it is controlled and limited so that it does not threaten the certainty of the group's beliefs.

The speculative nature of religion is likewise the reason that the bulk of religious scholarship is historically focused. Religious scholars predominantly do not focus on purely constructive work. The constructive work that is done is largely apologetic, seeking to justify some past way of thinking. In effect, religious scholars spend much time talking about what other people believe, but they devote relatively little energy to constructing a basis for religious belief that is empirically grounded. Compare this to the empirical sciences themselves. Researchers in these areas overwhelmingly concentrate on testing and advancing current theories. Much less time is spent trying to figure out exactly what scientists from the past thought, and scientists do not feel the need to necessarily justify new theories by showing that they are somehow consistent with past theories. It is simply accepted that past theories become outdated and, although we build on them in some way, we are not required to continually revere them or accord them any particular level of authority.

I would suggest that this neglect by religious scholars is ultimately attributable to the fragility of religious belief itself. Many religious beliefs would collapse like houses of cards if they were scrutinized to a significant degree. Throughout history those who questioned religious belief in a critical way often moderated or changed their views, since the beliefs could not withstand scrutiny. As defenders of their traditions, religious scholars must too frequently devote their skills to propping up the houses of cards. This is what Kant essentially argues when he says that historical, ecclesial faith requires much scholarship to support it. The more speculative the religious beliefs are, the more scholarship is required to provide an intellectual rationale for them. This is not to say that religious scholars do not help to promote intellectual progress. However, this progress is often marginal since religious scholars are burdened with the albatross of working under broad assumptions for which there is little basis. For example, how much more might Latter Day Saints scholars be able to achieve if they did not have to reconcile their beliefs with the Book of Mormon?

In a basic sense, we can define certainty as being convinced of the trustworthiness of our beliefs. It is regarding them as reliable. We want to be able to trust them so that we may put them to use and base other beliefs on them. The interesting thing is that trusting our beliefs ultimately entails trusting our own judgement. This does not mean that certainty is possessed only by those who are self-reliant, because time and time again we depend upon the thinking of others in forming our beliefs, and we can be just as certain of these beliefs as we can of those we construct for ourselves, sometimes even more so. However, certainty is ultimately a matter of trusting one's own judgement. Even the decision to trust the thinking of others is a matter of judgement. In other words, if I trust the beliefs of others, I am still making a judgement that *their* beliefs are trustworthy.

Certainty itself is thus tied to our self-esteem to some extent. Feeling good about our beliefs helps us to feel good about our ability to reason and make decisions. Inversely, it is difficult to be confident about our own thinking if we are uncertain about our beliefs. Nevertheless, this does not mean that the confident person sees a clear-cut answer to every question. Some questions do not have clear-cut answers, and it is quite feasible to be confident about this fact. Consequently, having certainty in our beliefs affects our self-esteem to the extent that we have *informed opinions* about various issues. Self-confidence is frequently thwarted whenever we lack informed opinions, because it forces us to stumble blindly along, either unduly trusting the thinking of others or accepting the vulnerability of ignorance.

EXTREMES TO BE AVOIDED

There are three extremes with regard to the certainty of beliefs. The first of these is *naiveté*. The naive are not really concerned with certainty, because they do not care about the trustworthiness of their beliefs. They are willing to accept them at face value. The second extreme of certainty is *scepticism*. Attaining certainty is not a priority for sceptics, because they deny the possibility of any significant degree of certainty. I should note here that the term *sceptic* and its variations (i.e. *sceptical, scepticism*) are sometimes used to denote the presence of doubt. I am using these terms in their stronger sense, indicating a level of doubt sufficient to significantly hinder belief if not preclude it altogether. The third extreme with regard to the certainty of beliefs is *dogmatism*. Certainty is of the utmost importance to dogmatists. Unfortunately, they are too certain of their beliefs, and so they fail to question them sufficiently (if at all). We will take a few moments to look at each of these extremes a little more closely.

Naiveté

When we speak of naiveté, we are referring to more than mere ignorance. Since none of us is omniscient, we are all ignorant in the sense that we still have more to learn. This is not naiveté. Instead, naiveté is being ignorant of several specific things with regard to knowledge. First, the naive are ignorant of *their own ignorance*. They simply do not realize how much they do not know. For years I heard a number of Christians depict education as the bane of Christian faith, because they believed that education ultimately turns people into haughty know-it-alls. Admittedly, I have found some individuals that fit into this generalization, because they were not interested in learning for the sake of discovering truth. What they really wanted to do was to bolster their own egos, and education merely became a means to this end. These people remind me of several young men I once knew who became overconfident after taking karate lessons for several months. Needless to say, they painfully became aware of the error of their ways. In reality, some of the best-educated individuals that I have met have also been the most humble, because education pursued for its own sake has a way of revealing to us the depths of our ignorance. No matter how much we learn, we discover that there is still much more that we do not know.

The second type of ignorance associated with naiveté is closely tied to this, namely an ignorance of *our own epistemic limitations*. This goes deeper than a knowledge of our own ignorance. Recognizing our epistemic limitations involves an awareness of our ability to discover and understand truth. In other words, I must realize my own fallibility, and this will prevent me from attaching too much confidence to my beliefs. Even when I am very informed and confident in my beliefs, I should appreciate the fact that I am always susceptible to error and misunderstanding. I should also keep in mind that others have the same foibles, so I should be careful not to put too much stock in the thinking of others either.

Third, the naive are ignorant of the *complexity of matters*. They tend to oversimplify issues, and they customarily resent those who challenge their simplicity. The naive thus characteristically see matters as 'black and white', so to speak, since they are unaware of the 'grey areas'. They do not understand how others could come to conclusions that differ from theirs. From their point of view, answers to problems are plain and simple. Anyone who sees things differently is suspected of being biased, because they believe that the truth is obvious to anyone who wishes to see it.

Some people actually choose to be ignorant and/or naive, because they do not want the responsibility of knowing the truth. They are content to live by the credo 'Ignorance is bliss.' In fact, many of the wilfully ignorant try to justify themselves by glorifying ignorance and disdaining knowledge. Those who do value knowledge and truth are ridiculed and shunned, and facts are ignored so that their false sense of security is not disturbed.

The two most common roots of naiveté are identified by Kant in his essay 'What Is Enlightenment?' The first one is *laziness*. Simply put, the naive are unwilling to investigate or wrestle with issues. They do not want to be bothered, and they do not wish to struggle with the doubts that often accompany the open pursuit of truth. The other common root of naiveté is *fear*, particularly a fear that one's beliefs will not withstand scrutiny or be able to compete with alternative theories. This reaction is actually well founded, because the naive typically do not have viable beliefs. Moreover, the naive many times lack the confidence to reformulate the beliefs that they fear are inadequate, so the fear is actually twofold.

Besides these two roots, there are additional causes which contribute to religious naiveté specifically. *Blind allegiance to tradition* is the first of these. Religious people revere their traditions to the point of regarding them as infallible guides. (This was discussed in the previous chapter.) In addition, *subjectivism* also contributes much to religious naiveté. Those who form their religious beliefs from a predominantly subjective point of view essentially minimize or reject all objective bases, including tradition. Indeed, they have very little desire to find any objective basis, because they do not see the need for one. Since religious beliefs are non-empirical and highly speculative, they can be somewhat impervious to attack as long as objectivity is not a priority. Religious beliefs that are subjective and naive can thus be insulated, providing their adherents with a hollow façade of certainty.

Scepticism

Since our knowledge is not perfect, any of it can be doubted. As Descartes pointed out, the only thing that cannot be denied at all is one's own existence. We know this just by the fact that we can think ('I think, therefore I am' – more commonly known as the *cogito*, taken from its Latin form 'Cogito, ergo sum'). Denying all else except for one's own existence is solipsism, and this is the most extreme form of scepticism. As I mentioned earlier, even the otherwise sceptical Hume admitted that we cannot function amid such overwhelming doubt. As G. E. Moore pointed out, radical scepticism eventually collapses upon itself. A number of postmodern thinkers have demonstrated this, for they assert that even dialogue itself is meaningless. These sceptics need to realize that knowledge can be relatively imperfect yet still be reliable. Rather than rule out the reliability of belief altogether, we should instead assess the reliability of our beliefs as best we can. This allows us to trust our beliefs at some justifiable level.

Religious scepticism rejects both objective and subjective bases for belief. It refuses to acknowledge any type of religious belief, so the particular basis that is given is rather inconsequential. There are many religious sceptics who simply set very high standards for belief and knowledge. In their opinion, the metaphysical nature of religious belief disqualifies it from consideration from the start. Radical empiricists like the logical positivists certainly fit into this category, and some of them went so far as to claim that they had eliminated metaphysics altogether. However, it cannot be denied that such antagonism towards religious belief is sometimes driven by personal animus. People may have some type of resentment against religion or religious people, or they may not want to feel obligated to conform to transcendent realities and values. Their judgement becomes skewed by these aversions. Nevertheless, whenever we encounter religious scepticism, it is a mistake to naturally assume that it is fuelled by animosity. Some people simply set the standard for belief very high, and this makes them less willing to trust as they are forming their beliefs.

For instance, Richard Dawkins rejects belief in God based on a probabilistic argument. He argues that the existence of God is extremely unlikely, if not altogether impossible. According to Dawkins, life appeared through the mechanism of natural selection, not through sheer chance. Natural selection essentially functions as a guiding mechanism by choosing traits individually, and this allows the improbability of life to be overcome gradually. It could be compared to discovering a secret password one character at a time, instead of randomly tryng entire combinations of characters. Nevertheless, Dawkins argues that it is even more unlikely that life arose from the intelligent design of God, since the probability is much lower that there is a being who made sure that all of the conditions necessary for life were met. However, Dawkins overlooks the fact that our existence raises this probability dramatically. In other words, a great part of Dawkins' improbability of God's existence is the improbability of our existence. Given the one (since we are here), the other becomes that much more likely.

Besides, no argument can actually make the existence of God improbable overall. All that can ever be asserted is that a particular type of God becomes less probable. For example, a typical complaint is 'How could God let my baby be killed like that? There surely is no God!' In reality, the possible existence of God is not diminished at all. What becomes evident, however, is that there is not a God who prevents babies from being killed. If God does exist, I cannot expect God necessarily to intervene if my baby's life is at risk. That has been rendered improbable by particular experiences.

In the final analysis, excessive scepticism in the realm of religious belief is largely misplaced, because we have only two ways to assess the probability of propositions, and they do not permit us to dismiss certain propositions like the basic existence of God. We rely on empirical data and logical reasoning, and these two things will not establish or eliminate the existence of God, nor will they make it more or less likely. At best, they can help us to determine what kind of God probably exists (if one exists at all). The existence of God is metaphysical and consequently beyond our limits of perception. If God is revealed to us, it must be within our limits of perception, but the question then arises whether the phenomena through which we believe that God is revealed are anything more than mere phenomena after all. That is the metaphysical question which ultimately cannot be answered by us, because our perception does not extend into that realm, despite the claims that many make in that regard.

Dogmatism

Whenever people are too certain of the truthfulness of their beliefs, they become unwilling to consider the possibility that they might be mistaken. Rather, they are convinced that everyone else is wrong. There are several factors which contribute to the unwarranted certainty of dogmatism. First, dogmatists are often in a state of *ignorance*. They are overconfident simply because they are unaware of the shortcomings of their views. They see issues simplistically, and they accuse others of complicating what seems obvious to them. In this way, dogmatists can be in a state of naiveté. There is thus nothing to prevent the naive from being dogmatic about their beliefs. Indeed, since they have no solid basis for their beliefs, the naive must be dogmatic if they want to feel certain about their beliefs to any significant degree.

Sometimes dogmatism can be motivated by a *fear of being wrong*. These dogmatists really are aware of the fallibility of their beliefs, but they refuse to accept this, so they compensate for their fears with excessive confidence. It might be understood as a state of denial. What they are denying are their own epistemic limits, and they do this by aggressively asserting the correctness of their beliefs. In essence, the rationale is that the best defence is a strong offence, because this type of dogmatism is actually a defensive mechanism.

Another common factor in dogmatism is *arrogance*. Some dogmatists are too proud to admit their own ignorance. They are very self-assured, and they are overconfident in their own judgements. In the worst cases, they do not respect the opinions of others. Just as they place too much confidence in themselves, they place too little confidence in others. Sadly, they never benefit from the opinions of others, because they are not interested in dialogue. Instead, their one concern is to convince others of their correctness.

In dogmatism, the stakes are higher because more is at risk. In all beliefs, there is always the possibility of being embarrassed when we must admit that we are wrong. The embarrassment is even higher for dogmatists, since they are adamant about being correct. It is very important for them to be correct and to be certain of their beliefs. As a result, they stand to lose more if their beliefs are shown to be faulty. For many people, the embarrassment of admitting that they are wrong (or simply might be wrong) is lessened if they can admit their fault without any external pressure. However, dogmatists are by nature generally not inclined to scrutinize their own beliefs, and so it is commonly the case that their beliefs will only face criticism if it comes externally, either from others or from situations that they encounter. Furthermore, since dogmatists tend to place greater emphasis on orthodoxy (i.e. on holding correct beliefs), they frequently have a more elaborate belief system. Consequently, revising the belief systems of dogmatists is ordinarily more extensive. This makes the task of revision more difficult and raises the risk of embarrassment even further. Yielding an important belief gives dogmatists an unwelcome feeling of vulnerability, because they are accustomed to feeling absolutely certain about their beliefs.

Dogmatism seems to occur with religious belief more than it does with other types of belief. Since religious beliefs are beliefs about the sacred, they are often mistakenly regarded as sacred themselves. People who make this mistake regard it as morally wrong to question their religious beliefs. It is a kind of sacrilege. However, just as beliefs about absolutes are not themselves absolute, so beliefs about the sacred are not themselves sacred. The fact that they concentrate on the sacred does indicate that they should be taken seriously and that we should endeavour to refine and solidify them as much as possible. Nevertheless, this does not mean that they cannot be questioned. Indeed, since religious beliefs are truly important, it is all the more imperative that they be as reliable as possible. This is not achieved by artificially giving them an unjustified level of certainty. Rather, they should be questioned and tested even more in order to make them the best that they can be. As Kant put it, religious incompetence is the most harmful and degrading type of incompetence.

Religious dogmatists can have any number of bases for their beliefs, both objective and subjective. Their beliefs may even be well founded and reliable. The key is the fact that they are unwilling to recognize epistemic limitations. What is missing is an attitude of intellectual humility. This is the real antidote to dogmatism.

TRUST

Since all of our beliefs are fallible, they all require trust. The three extremes discussed above represent different attitudes towards trust itself. Sceptics are unwilling to trust in forming belief, and so they trust too little. They set their standards too high, because they would rather avoid the risk of error, even at the cost of eliminating beliefs that might otherwise be considered valid and reliable. In contrast, the naive are too willing to trust in forming belief, because they do not scrutinize their beliefs sufficiently, if at all. They place their trust rather indiscriminately, lacking an objective basis for their beliefs and for the trust that they place in them.

Dogmatists also place too much trust in their beliefs, but they do not necessarily do so indiscriminately like the naive. Their desire is simply to retain their cherished beliefs. As we have already noted, some dogmatists are naive, and they stubbornly hold onto their beliefs without any objective basis to support them. Indeed, they are perfectly happy to hold unsupported beliefs, and they may not even be concerned about whether or not these beliefs are true. Other dogmatists do recognize the importance of having a reliable basis for their beliefs, and they labour to protect and defend them. However, they do not acknowledge the fallibility of their beliefs, and they thus assume that the beliefs are true. Consequently, although these dogmatists try to be objective, they fail to be truly so, since they presume to already know the truth. Their pursuit of truth is biased. Rather than weigh evidence on its own merits, these dogmatists selectively trust evidence that supports their cherished beliefs, and they ignore evidence that opposes their beliefs. All the while, they remain blind to their own prejudices.

Dogmatists are therefore guilty of misplacing their trust, and since trust is not placed in the proper places, this ultimately results in placing too much trust in other places. Consider the following example. Jane has been diagnosed with cancer, and her oncologist is proposing a treatment of radiation and chemotherapy. However, Jane also consults a holistic healer who advises against this, insisting that her cancer can be overcome through nutrition, etc. She must decide where she will place her trust. If she does not trust the doctor and the holistic healer appropriately, she will essentially be trusting one too much and the other too little. This is always the outcome of misplaced trust.

This can work in the opposite direction as well. Dogmatists often place too much trust in the sources of their beliefs, and this essentially means that their trust is misplaced. When too much trust is placed in one source, too little trust is being placed elsewhere. This kind of imbalance can happen when the sources of beliefs are regarded as sacred (e.g. Scripture and tradition). For instance, many fundamentalists refuse to accept evolution simply because they believe that Scripture can only be regarded as divinely inspired if it is historically accurate. Since they place too much trust in the historical accuracy of the biblical narratives of creation, they cannot trust science sufficiently. Consequently, their trust is misplaced.

Even though the results are basically the same in this instance as they are in Jane's decision, the dynamics are somewhat different. If Jane misplaces her trust, she does so unintentionally, because she really wants to determine the best way to treat her cancer. She is not dogmatic, and so she can possibly see her error at some point and correct it then. In contrast, dogmatists (like the fundamentalist creationists) do not want to know the truth. They would rather maintain their beliefs whether they are true or not. Their misplaced trust is consequently more intentional, even if it is due in part to ignorance. As long as they value belief more than truth, they will not admit their errors, much less correct them.

Once again, dogmatists as a matter of course place too much trust in their ability to form beliefs. They do not recognize their own fallibility, and they do not respect the ability of others to form beliefs. Instead, they assume that they are correct and their opponents are all wrong. This arrogance is also a type of misplaced trust. They trust themselves too much and others too little. We have already noted that we cannot claim absolute certainty for our beliefs. However, this does not require us to become radically sceptical either. Rather, it is important that trust be placed in a justifiable manner. There must be a reliable basis for trust, and the amount of trust placed must be proportionate to that reliability.

CERTAINTY AND DOUBT

In terms of certainty and doubt, the extremes must be avoided here as well. Navigating the waters between excessive certainty and excessive doubt requires several things. First, there must be a *desire to discover and embrace truth*. We cannot make belief more important than truth. Instead, we must value truth first and foremost, and our beliefs must hence be accountable to truth.

Second, we need to *recognize our own epistemic limitations.* In essence, our attitude should be one of humility. It is not shameful to admit our imperfections. Indeed, it is unacceptable to fail to do so.

Third, there must be a *willingness to trust* reliable sources of belief. There cannot be a bias against belief. The mere fact that something cannot be proven does not necessarily disprove it either. The matter must remain open to investigation.

Fourth, we ought to possess an *openness to changing our beliefs.* This includes a commitment to revising our beliefs as necessary. In essence, this merely carries the desire for truth even further.

Fifth, we must be *willing to live with some doubt.* Just as a willingness to trust is necessary to prevent excessive scepticism, a willingness to live with doubt is necessary to prevent excessive, false certainty.

Instead of resorting to one of the extremes, we must realize that certainty varies in degree according to the likelihood of the belief in question. At the one end of the spectrum is a high level of certainty. In these cases, we may not foresee any reason to doubt the beliefs in question, but we are still willing to do so as necessary. Such high certainty cannot become a type of absolutism, but must still admit the possibility of being wrong. At the other end of the spectrum is ambivalence. This is not radical scepticism, because there is a willingness to believe if there is enough basis to believe. In effect, this end of the spectrum is not the rejection of a belief. Rejecting a belief is essentially believing its opposite, and so certainty applies to the rejection of a belief just as it applies to its acceptance. We can be very certain or very ambivalent about accepting beliefs, and we can be very certain or very ambivalent about rejecting them, too.

Certainty and doubt are only proper when they are held in tension and keep one another in check. Certainty keeps doubt from stifling or precluding belief. It keeps searching for reasons to believe, and it uses doubt to test and evaluate those reasons so that they can be the best that they can be and thus maximize certainty. Conversely, doubt prevents certainty from making unfounded or excessive claims, and it does not allow certainty to become insulated and self-authenticating. Doubt uses certainty to build belief back up on a basis that is more reliable than its predecessor. At the end of the day, mature belief does not ignore or eliminate either certainty or doubt. Rather, it embraces both and uses them in tandem to establish and strengthen itself.

CHAPTER 11

FAITH AND BELIEF

FAITH AND REASON

All belief requires some degree of trust. At the very least, we must trust our senses and our ability to reason logically. The overwhelming majority of beliefs we hold require us to make inferences from more basic premises. As such, we place our trust in these inferences, and this is how belief originates. Since religious belief generally requires a higher level of trust than other types of belief, it is typically characterized as a matter of faith, even by religions themselves. The key issue with faith is the basis that supports it. In this book I have argued that belief should have a reliable basis, one that is as objective as possible. Within Christian circles the basis for Christian belief has traditionally been debated as the relationship between faith and reason, and this relationship has been construed according to the main epistemological theories that have prevailed in Western intellectual history.

Rationalism regards certain truths as logically necessary. A well-known example of Christian rationalism is Anselm's ontological argument for the existence of God. This proposes that since God surpasses all we can conceive, it is contradictory to assert that we can conceive God without him actually existing. Although some still find this argument compelling, most philosophers have rejected it for various reasons. The ontological argument illustrates how rationalists base faith on premises that they feel are logically necessary. Critics of rationalism have contended that such arguments are little more than sophistry, i.e. they sound convincing because of their complexity, but in reality they are largely speculative and have no substantial basis to support them. Rationalists indeed believe that faith and reason are compatible, but they are only able to make this connection by regarding unfounded, speculative claims as rational. In other words, it is easier to believe that religious belief is rational if you are willing to allow more things to count as rational.

Pragmatism teaches that something is true to the extent that it is useful, either personally or more broadly. The glaring weakness with this approach is its subjectivism. Interestingly enough, pragmatism did not really start out that way. One of the key founders of pragmatism was Charles Sanders Peirce, and his thought can actually be regarded as a non-foundationalist form of empiricism. Peirce's philosophy had an impact on the psychologist William James, who subsequently misconstrued Peirce's thought and essentially made pragmatism more subjective. James had a famous running debate with William K. Clifford over the justification of belief. Clifford argued that it is unethical to believe something without sufficient evidence, and this is generally limited to empirical data. For him, religious belief cannot be justified due to the fact that it lacks a strong empirical basis. Clifford's position is known as *strong justification*. In contrast, James defended what is referred to as *weak justification*. He asserted that we are justified in holding beliefs so long as there is not enough evidence to refute them. This entire debate ultimately boils down to a decision as to how objective and subjective we want our beliefs to be. I have argued throughout the book that belief should have a reliable objective basis, and this effectively eliminates pragmatism as a viable option, at least the subjectivist stripe popularized by James.

Existentialism, especially as it is expressed in religious belief, is likewise too subjective, because it predominantly views faith and belief as embracing the absurd (or as embracing 'nothingness'). Although existentialism is much more sophisticated than pragmatism, it is also more subjective, since pragmatism is at least based on empirical evidence. In contrast, the frame of reference in existentialism is inner consciousness. For that reason, existentialism is very beneficial in understanding matters from a psychological perspective. However, it is intentionally subjective. To be sure, some existentialists believe in some type of absolute reality, and this allows some place for objectivity. Nevertheless, the absolute of existentialism is typically regarded as wholly transcendent, so our perception of it is wholly subjective. In the end, existentialism is even more subjective than either rationalism or pragmatism, and it is only a step away from utter relativism, expressed most clearly in the *postmodernism* of today.

Empiricism is perhaps the epistemological theory most concerned with objectivity. It asserts that beliefs must be based on evidence, but not just any evidence is acceptable. Empiricists believe that the most reliable source of information we have is sensory perception, because sensory data is continually reinforced throughout our conscious moments. In fact, empiricists typically regard all knowledge as being rooted in sensory perception, and this effectively eliminates all other possible sources of knowledge. Since beliefs must be based on empirical data, this permits us to verify and test them. The problem with using empiricism as a framework for religious beliefs is that the two things are not really compatible, since they focus on different realms. Empiricism is limited to the physical world, which must be perceived through our senses. In contrast, religion deals with the metaphysical, i.e. that which lies beyond or beneath the physical. Strict empiricists (like the logical positivists) thus regard metaphysics as sheer speculation, due to the fact that they do not acknowledge anything other than sensory perception as a basis of knowledge. It is easy to see how empiricism and religious belief run in opposite directions. The more closely we adhere to one, the more we restrict the other.

RECONCILING THE EMPIRICAL WITH THE METAPHYSICAL

It is not only empiricists who recognize the role of the senses in the formation of beliefs and the establishment of knowledge. Most non-empiricists (excluding sceptics and radical mystics) do appreciate the importance of empirical data. They simply allow other sources and criteria to be a part of the process. Consequently, many people recognize the need to reconcile religious belief with empirical data in some way. Quite often this results in dividing faith and reason into separate spheres, relegating faith to the realm of the unknown. A great chasm is created between human knowledge and divine truth. According to this Platonic way of framing the issue, human knowledge (i.e. that which is empirically based) only takes us so far, so God must reveal his truth to us in supernatural ways, and we can only perceive it mystically. Someone will point out that our study and understanding of Scripture is empirical. However, the belief that the text itself is divinely inspired is premised upon the notion that the authors received some kind of mystical knowledge or insight. At the very least, their reasoning powers would need to be supernaturally heightened, allowing them to transcend the confines of their natural, empirical knowledge.

In effect, mysticism attempts to bridge the gap between the empirical and the metaphysical, between the natural and the supernatural, between the material and the spiritual. However, mystical experience is subjective, and so its claims of supernaturally imparted knowledge carry little weight with those who do not otherwise find relevance in the message that is being disseminated. As a result, mystical experience is often validated by miracles, i.e. supernatural acts that do not follow the normal, natural course of events. After all, miracles are inferred from empirical observation, and this seemingly gives some objectivity to the mystical revelation.

Nevertheless, these 'miraculous' events must defy scientific explanation if they are to have any metaphysical significance. After all, if the events can be explained scientifically, then presumably they no longer indicate special supernatural activity. (However, this does not indicate that there is no divine activity whatsoever. God may very well be working in covert ways.) Consequently, mysticism has historically engendered an attitude of anti-intellectualism, especially with regard to empirical science. Intellectual progress in effect undermines this type of faith by moving matters from the realm of the unknown to the domain of knowledge. In order to protect mystical faith, intellectual progress must be controlled and stifled when necessary. Claims to knowledge which oppose the 'mystical knowledge' must likewise be discredited if this faith is to remain secure. This is the typical and unfortunate result of relegating faith to the realm of the unknown.

In the eighteenth century there was a general trend of applying Lockean empiricism to other areas of belief. For example, a number of British moral philosophers suggested that conscience functions like a 'moral sense', enabling us to make moral judgements. Most of these theories combined empirical observation with intuition, and they varied in their objectivity and subjectivity. Carrying this trend even further, Jonathan Edwards and John Wesley attempted to apply their otherwise empiricist epistemology to spiritual matters, and they surmised that Christians must receive a 'spiritual sense' at the time of conversion that allows them to perceive spiritual truths and realities. Since this approach ventures further into the domain of the metaphysical, it is much more intuitive and subjective, if not altogether mystical. As a result, both Edwards and Wesley had to bolster their theories with other empirical safeguards. For instance, although Wesley claimed that Christians can 'feel' that their sins are forgiven through the 'direct witness of the Spirit', he subsequently added that this is reinforced through the more empirical 'indirect witness of conscience', in which notable changes in both attitude and lifestyle are observed.

All of this illustrates the subjectivity of mystical experience and the need to buttress it with empirical evidence, which is the only reliable basis of objectivity. Some people, in realizing this divide, essentially give up all hope of reconciling the empirical with the metaphysical, and they thus conclude that faith is illogical or paradoxical. However, I find the approach of Kant to be more practical. He expressed a desire to limit knowledge in order to allow room for faith. He felt that there is plenty of room for a rational faith in the metaphysical so long as epistemic limits are recognized. On one hand, this acknowledges the constraints of empirical observation. All of us perceive things from our own perspectives, and so all our beliefs and knowledge are fallible to some extent. Moreover, since the metaphysical realm lies beyond the empirical, metaphysics always remains a possibility to us and cannot simply be dismissed. On the other hand, metaphysics must then remain speculative. It cannot rise to the levels of certainty possible in empirical perception. We must ultimately not allow rationalism and mysticism to make unfounded metaphysical claims. At best, belief in the metaphysical can be rational yet tentative.

It is often argued that religion cannot be subject to science, but this is also an unfounded assertion, because all our beliefs should be empirically accountable, and the sciences (both natural and social) represent our best attempts to describe ourselves and the world in empirical terms. Granted, since science is dependent upon theories, it is also speculative to some degree, but not nearly as speculative as religion. For instance, can anyone honestly deny that the laws of thermodynamics are much less speculative than the Christian doctrine of the Trinity? Moreover, scientific theories are constantly being challenged and revised, because there is a concrete basis (i.e. empirical data) for doing so. Scientists thrive on disproving one another, because every successful challenge elevates the scientist and advances science. Religious belief lacks such an empirical basis, so it cannot be challenged as easily. Whereas science becomes more uniform over time, religion becomes increasingly fragmented.

Since it is wholly concerned with empirical data, science is more foundational than the more speculative disciplines like philosophy and theology. As such, philosophy and religion must be informed by science if they are to be intellectually credible and defensible. In turn, good science remains empirically grounded. It does not wander off into sheer speculation, but can only speculate in limited ways as it devises scientific theories. In contrast, religion speculates about higher-order questions that cannot be addressed empirically. It is fairly obvious that religion attempts to answer questions that are ultimately more important than those answered by science. Christian theology reached the zenith of its influence in the medieval period, when it was regarded as the 'queen of the sciences'. This appellation is appropriate in the sense that theology addresses the highest-order questions. Nevertheless, theology should serve this role by integrating all the disciplines of knowledge that are available to us.

Unfortunately, theology's role as 'queen of the sciences' has historically been falsely interpreted as a magisterium that trumps all else. In general, although religion focuses on life's most important questions, it remains highly speculative nonetheless, not being empirically based. The fact that its subject matter is more important does not make it more reliable or give it higher authority than other disciplines – that would be roughly the equivalent of using a more comprehensive but untested scientific theory to discredit and discard more basic theories that have already been shown to be reliable. It would also be like getting rid of trusty kitchen devices in order to use an all-in-one kitchen gadget that has not been tested. The reliability of religion cannot be established empirically, and so it remains highly speculative. The fact that it aims at absolute truth does not mean that it speaks with absolute truth.

In my opinion, religious dogmatists really do realize the fragility of their beliefs deep down, and this is evident in their self-serving use of science. Whenever science contradicts their dogma, they discredit it or put it in a separate (and lower) realm. Nevertheless, they are only too glad to use science when it appears to confirm their beliefs. For example, if scientists discovered evidence that suggested either that Jesus Christ lacked a biological father or that he really rose again from the dead, do we think that Christian theologians would ignore it and say that science has no bearing on the matter? Not at all! They would celebrate like never before. However, what if the opposite were true? Suppose the remains of Jesus Christ were unearthed and verified through DNA testing. What would the reaction be? Much different, I dare say!

Nobody can really blame religious dogmatists for not jumping on the bandwagon when new scientific theories appear. After all, the reliability of scientific theories needs to be established. However, how much evidence is enough? It seems that some people have decided what they want to believe, and they will continue to believe those things in spite of the evidence. How sad indeed! Truth gets subjugated to belief, and this is what stymies intellectual progress. This is what has happened historically whenever science has been subjugated to religion.

Faith attempts to reconcile the empirical with the metaphysical, but this should be done as objectively as possible. For too many religious people, the ends of belief really do justify using whatever means are necessary to sustain belief. If we are to attempt to be objective, we must be willing to accept the limitations of our beliefs and not ascribe to them certainty or reliability to which they are not entitled. Since religious belief is more speculative, religious faith requires a higher degree of trust than other types of belief. Nevertheless, this trust must continually remain aware of its own limitations and not become blind trust.

CHARACTERISTICS OF MATURE RELIGIOUS FAITH

In light of what has been said about faith, we can now identify some characteristics of mature faith. To start, it is imperative that faith *recognize its own fallibility*. It cannot irresponsibly make claims for which there is no reliable basis. Instead, a mature faith realizes the limits of knowledge and belief and always attempts to stay within those boundaries. Nevertheless, it is *not intellectually indifferent, but values truth*. Belief cannot be allowed to become more important than truth itself. The pursuit of truth must ultimately determine what we believe, why we believe it, and whether our beliefs need to be reconsidered. In that regard, since mature faith aims at knowing truth, it is always *willing to question its own beliefs*, at least to the extent that beliefs are not held with undue certainty. Since our beliefs are all fallible, absolute certainty is ruled out from the start, and there must always be an openness to reconsider our beliefs and to change them accordingly. Beliefs should stand on their own merits, rather than be artificially propped up by us. The more reliable our beliefs are, the less susceptible they will be to doubt, because the reliability of beliefs is often revealed by questioning and testing them. Beliefs that stand up to scrutiny are the ones that show themselves to be reliable.

Of course, *mature faith avoids the extremes of certainty: naiveté, scepticism and dogmatism.* A number of Christians erroneously claim that Jesus taught that we are to have 'childlike' faith, but this is not what the Bible conveys. Matthew 18.3–4 says that we must enter the kingdom of heaven as children, but this does not imply that we are to remain immature. Moreover, this passage indicates that we are to be like children in humility, not in our thinking. In fact, the New Testament is replete with passages that stress the opposite, i.e. the need to be mature in thought, putting away childish ways of thinking. In too many cases, the veneration of 'childlike' faith is just an excuse for irresponsibility, particularly with respect to intellectual maturity. People do not want to 'grow up' intellectually and accept responsibility for their beliefs. They are content either to uncritically accept what they have been taught or to just follow the herd.

In contrast, mature faith is driven by *independent thinking.* Maturity in general implies the ability and willingness to be responsible for oneself, and this cannot be accomplished at an intellectual level unless we are willing to think for ourselves. At the very least, we must want to have a rationale for our beliefs and not merely accept the beliefs that are given to us by others. Plainly and simply put, intellectual maturity cannot be attained by those who do not like to think for themselves. Nevertheless, it is foolish and arrogant not to be informed by the thinking of others, whether this stems from having too much confidence in our own abilities or too little confidence in the abilities of others. Mature faith thus has a *healthy dependence on the beliefs and opinions of others.* It does not accept what others say at face value, but it takes others seriously nonetheless. The intellectually mature consider all possible sources of knowledge and pursue those that offer the most promise of progress. Along those same lines, there must also be a *healthy dependence on our own beliefs.* We must indeed depend upon our beliefs, but whenever this dependence becomes too great, we will be less willing to relinquish our beliefs, even though other beliefs may indeed be more reliable.

The pursuit of truth is what ultimately causes mature faith to be *ever growing and changing*. Even if beliefs are not being replaced, the rationale for them is continually being developed. Consequently, mature faith constantly *desires to broaden its perspective and deepen its understanding*. The mature see the benefits of growth and hence see it as an adventure, not as a precipice. To be sure, we all differ in our ability to think through issues and seek answers to our questions, and so intellectual growth can be intimidating for many people. This is another reason why we must wisely rely on the thinking of others. We never outgrow this dependence altogether, even though it wanes as our own intellectual abilities increase. In a nutshell, life requires a certain amount of thinking, whether it is done by us or by others. The more we can think for ourselves, the less dependent we will be on the thinking of others. Inversely, the less we are able to think for ourselves, the more we must rely on the thinking of others. Since none of us is infallible, it is wise to utilize the thinking of others, and this must be done judiciously. Mature faith thus treads the waters between scepticism and dogmatism. It *places trust judiciously* in sources that can justifiably be regarded as reliable.

Those who are intellectually mature *do not require conformity of thought from others* but are *tolerant of different opinions*. Their desire is to discover and embrace truth wherever it is found. Since they are not concerned with protecting and defending their beliefs, they are not threatened by the beliefs of others. Instead, encountering the beliefs of others presents opportunities to explore their own beliefs in some way. Mature faith *seeks to understand, rather than fight or debate*. Nevertheless, once mature beliefs have faced particular challenges, facing the same challenges again will most likely not result in any real growth. As a result, the intellectually mature as a rule *benefit most from dialogue with others who are at least as mature as they are*. Our maturity is often reflected in the maturity of those who influence us.

As faith matures and grows in understanding, it increasingly *recognizes the complexity of issues*. The immature tend to oversimplify matters, because their perspectives are too limited. In contrast, the intellectually mature *give each possibility and each aspect due weight*. Nothing is ruled out without just cause. The more that mature faith takes into consideration, the more robust and reliable it becomes. It realizes the limits of belief and knowledge, and it consents to remaining within those limits. The intellectually mature are aware

FAITH AND BELIEF

that some issues cannot be resolved and thus remain open questions. In effect, mature faith is *willing to hold conflicting claims in tension*. It does not try to force a resolution between these points of tension. Rather, it accepts them as a part of the pursuit of truth. Mature faith thus *lives with a degree of doubt, in the twilight between certainty and scepticism*. It does not seek a false haven in any of the extremes, but it also does not allow the uncertainty of belief to become an excuse for intellectual laziness and irresponsibility. It continues to seek and to grow.

CHAPTER 12

CULTIVATING RELIGIOUS INTELLECTUAL MATURITY

TYPES OF RELIGIOUS INTELLECTUAL IMMATURITY

One aspect of immaturity is the inability to be responsible for oneself. Children are unable to take care of themselves, so they must depend upon others to take care of them. Along the same lines, the intellectually immature are unable, perhaps unwilling, to think for themselves, so they must rely upon others to think for them. They do not accept responsibility for their own beliefs or for the implications of their beliefs. Another aspect of immaturity related to this is the unwillingness to face reality and see things as they really are. The intellectually immature cannot handle the truth, and they are thus determined to defend the beliefs that they do not want to relinquish.

There are several ways of thinking that reflect these two aspects of immaturity to some extent. Adherents of these positions sometimes simply wish to avoid the responsibility of thinking. In other cases, they do not mind thinking about their beliefs per se, but they will only think about their beliefs in ways that do not seriously question them and put them at risk. In fact, people often spend a lot of time thinking up ways to defend their most cherished beliefs, but this is not motivated by intellectual honesty or by a sincere desire to discover truth. If we are to aspire to intellectual maturity, we must avoid these ways of thinking.

Superstition
Much religious belief throughout history has been little more than mere superstition. Religiously superstitious people essentially conclude that religious beliefs are beyond scrutiny. They cannot be evaluated on any objective basis, especially an empirical one.

Instead, things are viewed as magical, defying explanation. Mysticism often fits within this category, because it relegates much to the domain of 'mystery'. To be sure, all religious belief lies in the realm of the metaphysical and is largely shielded from empirical scrutiny, so there is no way to clearly demarcate a line dividing superstition from justifiable religious belief. Consequently, many critics characterize all religious belief as superstition, while many religious believers accept their superstitious beliefs as 'mystery', justified in the divine reason alone.

Since there is no sharp distinction between superstition and more legitimate kinds of religious belief, we must have criteria for judging the reliability of our religious beliefs, and I outlined some of these earlier. At the very least we should be able to recognize religious superstition wherever it appears. The term 'superstition' generally refers to counter-intuitive beliefs that rest on magical explanations. Superstitious religious beliefs thus *lack a sufficient objective basis*. Those who are more sceptical want to eliminate all religious superstition by limiting the objective basis for religious belief to that which rests directly upon empirical data. In contrast, others feel that any degree of objectivity is sufficient. They are satisfied to simply stop short of utter subjectivism. In other words, they are willing to accept the religious experiences of individuals as long as others make similar claims.

Although shared experience is certainly more objective than uniquely personal experiences, it cannot be denied that religious superstition is frequently shared by even large groups of people. Given the fact that religious beliefs cannot be refuted empirically, it is not surprising to observe members of religious groups sharing in common delusions. Indeed, each member's willingness to hold superstitious beliefs is strengthened by the willingness of other members to do the same. People assume that the greater the number of people who hold a particular belief, the more likely it is that the belief is true. This is a faulty assumption, and it is also a mistake to assume that the group will necessarily make steady progress and correct its errant beliefs.

As we have already seen, such progress is dependent upon the criteria that are used to evaluate belief. If the criteria never change but are consistently maintained, beliefs will tend to be reinforced, not undermined. The group will only abandon its superstitions if the criteria for belief are raised so as to eliminate this kind of belief. Since there is little within religion itself that would necessarily dictate such a change, the catalyst is often the desire of group members to more deeply integrate their religious beliefs with their other beliefs, and this sometimes takes a very long time, especially for people who tend to compartmentalize their beliefs, insulating their religious beliefs from criticism. In the final analysis, the immediate popularity of a particular religious belief in no way makes it any less superstitious. However, as people progress intellectually in other areas of their lives, their religious superstitions will eventually be abandoned to the extent that they want their religious beliefs to be commensurate with their other beliefs. For instance, most religious people have adjusted their beliefs about divine healing as medical science has progressed. In order to benefit from medical advances, their religious beliefs about healing have become less superstitious. Of course, there are still a few who superstitiously refuse certain kinds of medical treatment (e.g. operations and blood transfusions).

As I have already mentioned, there are those who want to eliminate all religious superstition by rejecting any belief that cannot be empirically corroborated. This will indeed eliminate superstition, but it will also eliminate the vast majority of religious beliefs altogether. Anyone who wants to remain open to the possibilities expressed by religion (e.g. God, spirit, afterlife) will not be satisfied with this approach. Nevertheless, if superstition is to be avoided, religious belief must be scrutinized to some extent. Anyone who wishes to steer clear of the extremes of scepticism and superstition must be aware of this and be willing to live with that tension. All religious belief tends towards superstition to some degree, and it must thus be kept in check through scrutiny and analysis.

Superstition often prevails whenever religion is allowed to trump all other claims to truth and knowledge. If superstition is to be minimized, religious belief must be accountable in some way, and the best candidate is in fact empirical data. Even if we do have other sources of information, it is clear that the senses are by far our most reliable source of information. We use them continually through all of our conscious moments, and they are ostensibly the foundation of an array of cognitive activities from common sense to science. Superstition ignores empirical data in favour of magical explanations. Therefore, much religious superstition can be eliminated by simply accepting explanations of events that are more obvious, reasonable and natural.

Overt superstition is perhaps the pinnacle of intellectual immaturity, because it wants to believe but not know. People who are blatantly superstitious do not desire to justify their beliefs in any objective way. As a result, religious superstition too often is just an easy excuse for avoiding intellectual responsibility. Superstitious beliefs end up being justified by further superstitions, as the criteria for belief are lowered further and further. Whenever adequate boundaries are not maintained for religious belief, superstition is frequently the result. As the boundaries are minimized, superstitious beliefs end up being inane, and this exposes the intellectual immaturity of those who embrace them.

Authoritarianism

Throughout history religious beliefs have often been accepted on the basis of religious authority. Regardless of the legitimacy of religious authority, the fact is that authoritarianism perpetuates intellectual immaturity. It not only teaches people to allow others to think for them, but it also regards it as virtuous to do so. People are discouraged from thinking for themselves, and when they begin to accept this, they no longer feel responsible for their own beliefs. Instead, they place their fate in the hands of the religious hierarchy, and they stop growing and developing intellectually.

In authoritarianism a few select people think for the group. If these few are highly qualified to do so, then this can be a reasonable option. However, the benefit of having a few qualified individuals think for the group is limited. First, overall progress is maximized whenever there is a larger pool of thinkers. No individual, no matter how qualified, is infallible. As such, there is intellectual strength in the free exchange of ideas. Second, giving control to a select few only perpetuates the intellectual immaturity of the group at large. People cannot mature intellectually until they learn to think for themselves. In that regard, it is important to note that intellectual maturity is not merely being able to think for oneself, it is being able to think well. Many people think for themselves, but their thinking is certainly nothing that should be lauded or emulated. Nevertheless, being able to think for oneself is a prerequisite to intellectual maturity. Once we become responsible for our own thinking, it is able to develop and mature.

Religious groups try to elevate their leaders in various ways. They are frequently given special titles, they might don special apparel, and they are sometimes granted prophetic status. Some Christian denominations in the United States use their own educational institutions to grant honorary doctorates to their elected officials. Of course, they wish to honour their leaders, but it seems rather obvious that there is also a desire to make the leaders look more intellectual. In this way, dogmatists display a love–hate relationship with scholarship. In nearly Machiavellian fashion, they want to appear scholarly, but they recoil from actually engaging in critical scholarship to the extent of allowing their cherished beliefs to be questioned or placed at risk.

Emotionalism

Some people remain intellectually immature because they are slaves to their emotions. For them happiness is the most important thing, and they do not want to sacrifice it. Understanding truth is not a great priority for them. Rather, they construct their own reality in order to maintain happiness. Granted, emotionalism is not always utterly subjective. As long as it contributes to their happiness, emotionalists will try to be objective. However, happiness generally takes precedence over objectivity since it is the highest priority. Emotionalists typically sacrifice objectivity in order to preserve happiness. They are unwilling to face reality and be fully responsible. Consequently, their ignorance really is bliss.

Notwithstanding, the dichotomy between the head and the heart is a false one. Emotions are not antithetical to reason, so pursuing intellectual maturity does not destroy emotional enjoyment. To be sure, shattering false hopes and expectations will reduce one's immediate happiness, yet this does not prevent other types of happiness from replacing the obsolete hopes. We can replace fleeting types of happiness with more reliable, more substantial types of happiness. Rather than sabotage the emotions, intellectual maturity results in emotional maturity as well. As emotions deepen they become steadier and more stable, and they are actually less vulnerable than shallow emotions. The trade-off is that mature emotions usually do not achieve the peaks and troughs of immature emotions. This is why emotionalists avoid intellectual maturity. They are too dependent upon the emotional highs to which they are accustomed.

Dogmatism

Dogmatism is really in a separate class by itself, because it is a general attitude towards belief that can be applied to all belief systems. Any belief can be held dogmatically, i.e. it can be embraced with too much certainty. As such, dogmatists exhibit varying degrees of intellectual maturity. The very immature can be dogmatic about their beliefs, and those who are more mature can also be dogmatic. However, dogmatism itself prevents people from maturing fully, because it represents an unwillingness to go beyond a certain point of questioning. For example, fundamentalism asserts that there are particular 'fundamentals' which cannot be questioned or sacrificed. At the point where questioning belief is no longer allowed, the emphasis shifts from discovering truth to defending belief, and this is where maturing stops.

Some dogmatists are satisfied with simplistic answers. They do not demand much of a basis for their beliefs. Other dogmatists engage in apologetics, because they set higher standards for their beliefs. Since they have already concluded that their beliefs are true, they are not interested in evidence that challenges them. Instead, they seek out evidence that supports their beliefs. Of course, as the amount of counter-evidence mounts up over time, the task becomes increasingly difficult and the explanations naturally become increasingly convoluted. It is thus wise to apply Ockham's Razor, which states that it is best to use the simplest adequate explanation. After all, there is a certain freedom in being willing to face the truth, because there is no longer a need to defend our beliefs at all costs. This freedom is one of the rewards of intellectual maturity.

SAFE HAVENS FOR RELIGIOUS INTELLECTUAL IMMATURITY

There are several intellectual frameworks that offer a place of refuge for the intellectually immature. They are not necessarily immature ways of thinking. The immature are attracted to them because they help to legitimate the beliefs that the immature hold. The more sophisticated the framework, the more legitimate the beliefs seem to be. The key thing is that these ways of thinking help the immature to avoid responsibility for their beliefs, since they would appear to obviate the need for the immature to evaluate and justify their own beliefs.

Rationalism
In rationalism, some matters are regarded as intuitive, self-evident or logically necessary. As such, these matters do not need to be

justified or scrutinized empirically. The intellectually immature put their trust in these arguments in order to give credence to their beliefs. They may not even understand the arguments, but they are willing to trust the arguments and those who advance them. However, in many cases this trust is placed primarily as a matter of convenience. People pick and choose the rationalistic arguments that support their particular beliefs. They do not feel compelled to consider counter-arguments, nor do they see the need to seriously evaluate other arguments posed by these same thinkers. In fact, it is common for the intellectually immature to stand behind arguments advanced by thinkers of whom they know very little or with whom they have no other points of agreement. Credibility is not an issue with them. It is sufficient to hear these thinkers coming to the same conclusions as them, even if they do not understand how these conclusions are reached.

For example, consider the classic arguments to support, demonstrate or otherwise prove the existence of God – for example, the ontological argument and Aquinas's Five Ways. Many people who believe in the existence of God feel reassured by these arguments, even though they are unable to assess the strengths and weaknesses of these positions. Along similar lines, the intelligent-design theories try to show the logical necessity of a Creator in the process of evolution. Many advocates of these theories have very little idea of the complexities that are involved, yet it gives them peace of mind to think that their views have been validated in a more sophisticated way.

An intriguing example is religious existentialism. In my opinion, many people within this camp are oblivious to the nuances of existentialist philosophy. However, that does not stop them from appropriating the concepts and terminology in order to justify their own beliefs. For the intellectually immature, existentialism is often nothing more than a sophisticated form of utter subjectivism. It gives them some intellectual ground to stand on while they avoid facing tough empirical questions, made possible by the sharp divide that existentialism makes between the material world and the realm of consciousness. In a similar fashion, since phenomenology focuses on our inner, subjective perceptions, it is often used as a crutch to support good old-fashioned mysticism. It helps mystics to feel that there is an intellectual basis for their subjective religious experiences, which certainly cannot be justified empirically. At the end of the day, the concepts and terminology of phenomenology are used to rationalize some of the very things that the philosophy of phenomenology seeks to eliminate.

Pragmatism

The intellectually immature are attracted to the subjective type of pragmatism, like that espoused by James. They feel justified in holding beliefs as long as they continue to be personally useful. They see no need to examine these beliefs any further or seek an objective basis for them. On the positive side, basing religious beliefs on pragmatic considerations helps to keep them personally relevant. Each person essentially embraces a custom-made set of beliefs to fit his or her unique set of experiences. This pattern is especially evident in the United States, where the desire and freedom to keep religion practical and relevant has effectively splintered and divided religious groups time and time again.

On the negative side, this approach permits virtually any religious belief that is coherent and provides a benefit, which could be any number of things. Religious beliefs quite often serve a psychological function, giving people meaning, purpose and hope, as well as a framework for coping with the problems of life. They are also a means of group identification, uniting particular individuals. In fact, religious beliefs serve a variety of functions that are all certainly worthwhile, and this makes it tempting to base religious beliefs on subjective pragmatism.

However, whenever we realize just how many religious beliefs can satisfy these criteria, the result is staggering. It is even quite intimidating to think that we might so easily justify religious beliefs that cannot be refuted or disproven. At best, such religious beliefs must be shown to be impractical if they are to be rejected, since objectivity is not really desired. As long as religious beliefs perform a function that keeps people rooted in reality, they are truly beneficial. Unfortunately, the subjective pragmatist basis allows people to construct their own fantasy worlds so that they will not have to face reality, and this is the appeal to the intellectually immature. They do not have to think issues through. Instead, they can simply build a wall of bogus religious beliefs around themselves, a wall that gives them their own alternative 'reality'. There are many people who thus consider their religious beliefs to be the 'real' or 'absolute' truth, even if they contradict empirical fact. Indeed, they use their personally constructed frame of reference to trump the real world.

This is nothing more than sheer intellectual immaturity, a type of escapism.

Radical scepticism

Those who are truly sceptics on philosophical grounds wrestle with epistemic issues and limits. They take these matters seriously, and they do not attempt to oversimplify them in any way. In contrast, the intellectually immature simply hide behind this scepticism in order to avoid intellectual responsibility. Rather than face the difficult issues, it is easier to dismiss them out of hand. A friend of mine recently told of how her sister lost her faith in God after personal tragedy. However, she was glad to report that her sister had begun to regain her faith after becoming involved in a prayer and Bible study group. It was clear to me that her sister's scepticism was not philosophical in nature. If it were, her faith would not have been recovered through prayer and Bible study, because philosophical scepticism would lead one to doubt the validity of these activities. No, she abandoned her faith in order to avoid facing the question of theodicy (i.e. why God allows bad things to happen). It was easier to make the question go away by denying the existence of God altogether. Immature belief changes quickly, and maturity is what stabilizes it and makes it more consistent. The longer it takes for faith to be lost, the less likely it is that it will be recovered, because the conclusions are formed after deliberation. For immature belief it is easy come, easy go (and vice versa).

Furthermore, scepticism often has a false appeal as an intellectually superior position. People see how intellectually flimsy naiveté is, and this makes scepticism appear intellectually sophisticated, as an opposite of naiveté. I once had a student who claimed that we cannot really know anything. Of course, I realize that a number of notable thinkers take this position, and I am aware of the arguments that they construct, but I was not convinced that this student really knew what he was talking about. Instead, it seemed that what he really wanted to do was to impress his friends and classmates. He also used his pseudo-intellectual status as an excuse for not completing assignments. In fact, whenever I require students to critique a particular text, I inevitably receive at least one essay that ignores the task by simply claiming that the entire assignment is a complete waste of time. They provide no details, just a knee-jerk reaction. They fail to understand that it is never a waste of time to read or listen to the opinions of others if we take the time to think about why we agree or disagree with them. The intellectually immature are only interested in conclusions, not in rationale, and so they only want to be exposed to opinions that come to the same conclusions that they embrace. Scepticism provides a convenient way to avoid considering opinions with which we do not agree.

In reality, scepticism is like all other epistemological positions in that it is no more sophisticated than the reasons for which it is embraced. Scepticism can be just as immature as other positions if it is comprised of simplistic beliefs that are not based on rational analysis. However, intellectually mature scepticism must be given due consideration. Criticism is ultimately an expression of belief, and it thus carries the force of the reasons that support it. A thoughtful critique must be given more weight than a superficial one. In the end, scepticism can provide useful criticism, but it also provides yet another way for the intellectually immature to justify shallow beliefs. Moreover, it gives them an intellectual framework for relativism and subjectivism. Scepticism is an easy way to avoid the tough struggles of intellectual maturity and eliminate all forms of intellectual accountability.

STEPS TOWARDS RELIGIOUS INTELLECTUAL MATURITY

Deepening understanding

Thinking that is intellectually immature tends to be shallow. Its rationale is weak, perhaps even illogical, and the basis for belief is rather superficial. Consequently, a critical part of the process of intellectual maturity is the deepening of the understanding. For the mature this is a natural part of thinking. They wish to go deeper and deeper in their beliefs, so the process includes an ongoing effort to discover and assimilate new information. As such, the mature constantly revise and replace their beliefs as necessary, and the immature must likewise be willing to do this if they are to progress towards maturity, especially since the immature typically have beliefs that are intellectually inadequate.

In order for this to take place, beliefs must be examined critically. At the very least this involves evaluating three things. First, we must consider criticisms that are levelled against our beliefs. Second, we need to be aware of alternative theories that compete with our beliefs. Essentially, our beliefs represent the conclusions that we have reached about the information we amass throughout our lives. Intellectual maturity involves an awareness of the different ways that this information can be interpreted. In other words, there is more than one way to interpret a given body of information, so a number of beliefs can be supported on the same basis. The intellectually mature thus have the ability to reinterpret their experiences and change their beliefs. Third, we must be willing to evaluate the basis for our beliefs, the criteria we use in forming beliefs.

It is most difficult to critically question the basis for belief. That requires even the criteria for judgement to be evaluated. This includes determining what is to be counted as evidence as well as how much weight to give each type of evidence. It is much easier to defend our beliefs by simply warding off criticisms that are levelled against them and criticizing theories that compete with them. Neither of these activities requires our criteria for belief to be questioned.

Consider the case of creation science, for instance. Creation science devotees routinely find ways to ward off the attacks that their beliefs encounter. For example, some of them appeal to the biblical account of Noah's flood in an attempt to rectify their highly dubious interpretation of the fossil record, while others conjecture that God may have created the world with fossil remains in it (in order to confound the sceptics). In general, constructing defences against attack is not that difficult, but the defences are frequently not any more intellectually sound than the beliefs themselves. In the same way, creation science supporters are skilled in attacking competing theories like evolution, because this is relatively easy to do. (However, their attacks are not that impressive either.) After all, it is much easier to find flaws or weaknesses in the arguments of others than it is to construct a flawless, invincible argument of one's own. The creation science advocates are much more willing to defend and attack than they are to reconsider the criteria by which they judge the fossil record, because this would also force them to change the criteria by which they judge the Bible.

Since religious belief is not primarily based on empirical data, it can withstand the first two types of challenges rather easily. Although our religious beliefs are largely speculative, criticisms of those beliefs likewise tend to be speculative, so they are more quickly dismissed. Alternative theories are also speculative, and there is typically no objective basis by which to arbitrate between them.

Consequently, it is rather obvious that a religion like Christianity will remain fragmented unless it either is controlled by a hierarchy or becomes so beholden to tradition that it ceases to change, in which case it would become intellectually stagnant. As long as religion is ultimately in the hands of the individual, it will be fragmented. Nevertheless, I am by no means suggesting that religion should be controlled externally. Instead, it must be controlled internally – by individuals themselves. The problem does not lie in the fact that religion is speculative. If people were willing to accept this fact, they would enjoy religious dialogue and not see opposing viewpoints as threatening. Rather, the problem stems from the desire that people predominantly have to try to deny the speculative nature of religion and to somehow regard it as absolutely certain. This impulse is the same one responsible for the tendency of religion to become dogmatic.

Dogmatists (e.g. fundamentalists) can engage in the first two types of evaluation but not the third, as we have already seen in the case of creation science. They can more easily ward off attacks and launch attacks of their own against competing theories. However, they will not criticize the criteria by which they form their beliefs, because this would threaten the beliefs themselves. As I have indicated throughout the book, this is the subjugation of truth to belief. For dogmatists it is more important to defend their beliefs than it is to discover truth. In effect, they are able to engage in scholarship without really being critical of their own beliefs. They just assume that the criteria by which they make judgements are valid. As long as they stay within those limits, they can consider all kinds of opinions, appropriating whatever they find helpful and dismissing the rest. Every source evaluated ultimately stands or falls based on how it measures up to the criteria that are used. Dogmatists also look for further evidence which will bolster their beliefs. They essentially follow the advice of the old song, 'You've got to accentuate the positive, eliminate the negative'.

In fact, dogmatists can be more widely read and be more heavily engaged in research than others who are more critical of their own beliefs. The more critical people are about what should be considered to be a proper basis for belief, the less evidence they will be willing to consider. Inversely, those who are less critical allow much more to count as evidence. They are thus more willing to consider a broader range of evidence. This can make dogmatists appear to be more objective and open-minded than those who are more sceptical. In reality, they simply have lower epistemic standards.

This is why it is really unnecessary for dogmatists to be anti-intellectual. Their beliefs will not falter but will actually be strengthened as long as their criteria for belief are not doubted and there is a modicum of evidence to support their beliefs (i.e. their beliefs are not ad hoc). With their criteria for belief intact, dogmatists can explore and investigate without fear, since the criteria will serve as a sieve to sift through information, incorporating that which is helpful and rejecting that which is potentially damaging. Consequently, intellectualism in general will not challenge dogmatism. A deeper level of scepticism is necessary, a level at which the very criteria for belief are challenged.

This is what Descartes believed, and he proposed that this kind of scepticism is healthy for belief. Otherwise, we may continue to live with various delusions. Our beliefs need to be questioned at a very basic level before we can truly have any significant amount of certainty about them. This theme was developed and applied throughout the Enlightenment, but not universally. While the empiricists became increasingly sceptical, the rationalists continued to cultivate speculative ways of thinking. At the same time, control shifted from hierarchies to the grass-roots population in many Christian groups, and they began to move away from controlled intellectualism towards fully fledged anti-intellectualism.

However, as the general population gradually became more educated, this anti-intellectualism could not be sustained without damaging the relevance and credibility of these groups, so they started to reverse the trend. First they founded Bible colleges, then these institutions predominantly became Christian liberal arts colleges, and now many of them are universities. There are even a select few that could be considered research universities of sorts. Nevertheless, since these traditions are dogmatic at their core, the shift has to a great extent been away from anti-intellectualism back to a controlled intellectualism. They have less difficulty appropriating speculative, rationalistic ways of thinking than they do reconciling their beliefs with empiricism, which is more sceptical by nature.

As a result, the heaviest clashes have come from interactions between theology and the empirical sciences. In places where science and theology are regarded as being in separate domains, the major difficulties are basically eliminated. In places where the desire is to integrate theology with other disciplines of knowledge, the conflict is governed by the level of dogmatism that is defended, and the empirical sciences represent one of the two greatest threats to dogmatic belief. The other threat comes from philosophy, which can be intimidating to dogmatists in two respects. Philosophy is effective at uncovering logical flaws and inconsistencies, and it can push scepticism to deeper levels. Both of these pose difficulties for dogmatism. Of course, some philosophers are less sceptical and more speculative than others, and those who are committed to religious dogma often engage in philosophy along these lines, if at all. In contrast, philosophers who are more sceptical are not likely to be dogmatic about their beliefs, especially those that are metaphysical or religious in nature. At the end of the day, whenever dogmatic theology clashes with either empirical science or philosophy, one must be compromised in order to preserve the other.

Most people are unwilling to live with the levels of uncertainty that are necessary for intellectual maturity. The exceptions to this are the postmodernists, some of whom take scepticism to more extreme levels. In my opinion, they take it too far, because they deny trust in many things that can generally be regarded as reliable. Rather than flatly reject the possibilities of acquiring truth or knowledge, we ought to measure all our beliefs by their reliability, but we can only do this to the depth of our understanding. In order to mature intellectually, we need to understand at a deeper level, and this will enable us to better assess the reliability of our beliefs.

Broadening perspective

In the same way, intellectual immaturity is often fostered by narrow thinking. The thinking of the immature is often confined to a limited range of exposure. They live in their own 'bubbles', so to speak. An important step in intellectual maturity is exposing ourselves to other ways of thinking. However, mere exposure will not guarantee maturity. Rather, we must allow the beliefs of others to challenge our beliefs so as to force us to have a better basis for them. This will spur us to either strengthen our beliefs or replace them with better beliefs.

In order for our beliefs to be challenged, the exposure we encounter must be to ways of thinking that are at least as mature as our own. It is rather obvious that intellectual challenges can only come from thinking that is superior to our own. However, if the gap is too great between our thinking and a new way of thinking, we will not be able to understand or appreciate that to which we have been exposed, and we will thus be unable to benefit from it. The challenges we receive must be still be accessible to us. Intellectual progress must therefore occur incrementally.

The upshot of this is that intellectual progress must be continual if it is to be significant. Granted, there are 'eureka' moments in our lives that seem to involve great intellectual leaps. However, these apparent leaps are not so much great advances in knowledge or complexity as they are the crossing of critical thresholds that open up new possibilities of thinking for us. For example, consider a child learning about human reproduction. The child has not suddenly gained a wealth of knowledge or become more intellectually sophisticated, but has discovered something important that will allow growth and development in ways that were previously inaccessible.

Of course, we must have a desire to face the challenges we meet and not simply dismiss new ideas without giving them due consideration. The exposure to new ways of thinking requires us to integrate more information and beliefs into our belief structure, and this is essentially what broadens our perspectives. This requires a deeper level of understanding, because the more information we must integrate, often the deeper we must go to find ways to relate the various concepts. Consequently, intellectual breadth and depth usually go hand in hand. They both need to be increased in the process of intellectual maturity.

Accountability and mentoring

Since we can learn from the mature thinking of others, accountability and mentoring are both key factors in the process. We can benefit from others by observing the ways that they think. As we begin to understand how they process information, this gives us options for processing information in our own thinking. Quite often it is helpful to hold a dialogue with others so that we can think alongside them. In addition, accountability to others (especially mentors) helps us to better assess our own thinking, because we are often blind to our own faults and shortcomings. We can thus benefit from the scrutiny of others.

There are several qualities that we should seek in our mentors. First, a good mentor is someone whose *thinking we admire*. In the process of mentoring we learn to think like our mentors. Indeed, this is how philosophy was done in ancient Greece, and this blueprint has been replicated many times ever since. Students learn to think like their teachers, and this shapes the development of their own unique perspectives. Second, effective mentors will *challenge our thinking*. They will not allow us to make unfounded assumptions but will require us to think more deeply and more broadly. Good mentors force their students to rethink matters that they have taken for granted. Third, mentors must be people that *we can trust*, since this will allow us to *have honest dialogue*. We can only grow in our thinking if we can be absolutely honest about our doubts, motivations, confusion, etc. Our thinking will never be able to develop if it is false in any way.

The immature are those who are dependent on others. They are unable to take care of themselves. As we mature, we develop in our own thinking, and we thus become less dependent on the thinking of others. However, since none of us is infallible, we all need to be accountable to others, and we can all benefit from the guidance of mentors, regardless of how sophisticated our thinking might become. Nevertheless, the highest level of maturity is being able to take care of others. This is the point at which the intellectually mature become mentors to others. We should all aspire to this and accept the mantle of intellectual leadership and influence whenever it is thrust upon us. Hopefully, we will appreciate the gravity of this responsibility and strive to keep maturing in our own thinking so that our influence on others will be positive and promote intellectual progress and maturity.

CONCLUSION

Just as Kant trumpeted the call to intellectual maturity, especially in matters of religion, I am thoroughly convinced that we need to cultivate religious intellectual maturity today. It is my sincere hope that this book has been beneficial in that regard. I have not tried to persuade readers to embrace or reject particular beliefs, but that is not because I do not have beliefs and opinions of my own. I am more interested in enabling and encouraging others to think for themselves. Kant said that religious incompetence is the most degrading of all, and that statement was made at the turn of the nineteenth century. One can only imagine what he might think of the state of religion today. We must have the courage to break free from the bonds of intellectual immaturity. We need to do this on an individual basis so that we might be able to lead others down the same path. May we all accept this challenge and press on to maturity.

RECOMMENDED READING

Ackerman, Robert J. *Belief and Knowledge*. Garden City, NY: Anchor Books, 1972.

Aquinas, St Thomas. *Summa Theologica*. 1911. Reprint, New York: Benziger Bros., 1948.

Armstrong, D. M. *Belief, Truth and Knowledge*. Cambridge: Cambridge University Press, 1973.

Audi, Robert. *Belief, Justification, and Knowledge: An Introduction to Epistemology*. Belmont, CA: Wadsworth, 1988.

Ayer, A. J. *The Problem of Knowledge*. New York: St Martin's Press, 1965.

Berkeley, George. *Principles of Human Knowledge*. 1710. Reprint, London: Penguin, 1988.

Blackburn, Simon. *Truth: A Guide*. Oxford: Oxford University Press, 2005.

Bowne, Borden P. *Theory of Thought and Knowledge*. New York: American Book Company, 1897.

Capaldi, Nicholas. *Human Knowledge: A Philosophical Analysis of Its Meaning and Scope*. New York: Pegasus, 1969.

Chisholm, Roderick M. *Theory of Knowledge*. Englewood Cliffs, NJ: Prentice Hall, 1966.

Clifford, W. K. *The Ethics of Belief and Other Essays*. Amherst, NY: Prometheus, 1999.

Cornforth, Maurice. *The Theory of Knowledge*. New York: International Publishers, 1955.

Dancy, Jonathan, and Ernest Sosa, eds. *A Companion to Epistemology*. Oxford: Blackwell, 1992.

Dawkins, Richard. *The God Delusion*. Boston, MA: Houghton Mifflin, 2006.

DePaul, Michael, and Linda Zagzebski, eds. *Intellectual Virtue: Perspectives from Ethics and Epistemology*. Oxford: Clarendon, 2003.

Descartes, René. *Discourse on Method*. 1637. Reprint, Mineola, NY: Dover, 2003.

——. *Meditations on First Philosophy*. 1641. Reprint, Mineola, NY: Dover, 2003.

Evans, C. Stephen, and Merold Westphal, eds. *Christian Perspectives on Religious Knowledge*. Grand Rapids, MI: Eerdmans, 1993.

Feldman, Richard. *Epistemology*. Upper Saddle River, NJ: Prentice Hall, 2003.

Fowler, James W. *Stages of Faith: The Psychology of Human Development and the Quest for Meaning*. San Francisco: HarperCollins, 1995.

Goldman, Alvin I. *Epistemology and Cognition*. Cambridge, MA: Harvard University, 1986.

Hamlyn, D. W. *The Theory of Knowledge*. Garden City, NY: Anchor Books, 1970.

Helm, Paul. *Faith Within Reason*. Oxford: Clarendon Press, 2005.

Hume, David. *An Enquiry Concerning Human Understanding*. 1777. Reprint, Indianapolis, IN: Hackett, 1993.

———. *Dialogues Concerning Natural Religion*. 1779. Reprint, Indianapolis, IN: Hackett, 1998.

———. *Treatise of Human Nature*. 1739. Reprint, Amherst, NY: Prometheus, 1992.

James, William. *The Meaning of Truth*. 1909. Reprint, Mineola, NY: Dover, 2002.

———. *The Varieties of Religious Experience*. 1902. Reprint, New York: Random House, 1999.

———. *The Will to Believe*. 1897. Reprint, Mineola, NY: Dover, 1956.

Kant, Immanuel. *Critique of Pure Reason*. 1787. Reprint, New York: St Martin's, 1929.

Kuhn, Thomas S. *The Structure of Scientific Revolutions*. Chicago, IL: University of Chicago Press, 1970.

Lehrer, Keith. *Self-Trust: A Study of Reason, Knowledge and Autonomy*. Oxford: Clarendon, 1997.

———. *Theory of Knowledge*. Boulder, CO: Westview Press, 2000.

Locke, John. *An Essay Concerning Human Understanding*. 1700. Reprint, Mineola, NY: Dover, 1959.

Moore, G. E. *G. E. Moore: Selected Writings*. Edited by Thomas Baldwin. London: Routledge, 1993.

Murphy, Nancey. *Theology in the Age of Scientific Reasoning*. Ithica, NY: Cornell University Press, 1990.

Nussbaum, Martha C. *Upheavals of Thought: The Intelligence of Emotions*. Cambridge: Cambridge University Press, 2001.

Peirce, Charles Sanders. *The Philosophy of Peirce: Selected Writings*. Edited by Justus Buchler. New York: Harcourt, Brace & Company, 1950.

Plantinga, Alvin. *Warranted Christian Belief*. New York: Oxford, 2000.

Plantinga, Alvin, and Nicholas Wolterstorff, eds. *Faith and Rationality: Reason and Belief in God*. Notre Dame, IN: University of Notre Dame Press, 1983.

Popper, Karl R. *Objective Knowledge: An Evolutionary Approach*. Oxford: Clarendon Press, 1972.

———. *The Logic of Scientific Discovery*. London: Hutchinson, 1959.

Reid, Thomas. *Essays on the Active Powers of the Human Mind*. 1788. Reprint, Cambridge, MA: MIT Press, 1969.

———. *Essays on the Intellectual Powers of Man*. 1785. Reprint, Cambridge, MA: MIT Press, 1969.

Roth, Michael D., and Leon Galis, eds. *Knowing: Essays in the Analysis of Knowledge.* New York: Random House, 1970.

Rubenstein, Richard E. *Aristotle's Children: How Christians, Muslims, and Jews Rediscovered Ancient Wisdom and Illuminated the Dark Ages.* Orlando, FL: Harcourt, 2003.

Russell, Bertrand. *Human Knowledge: Its Scope and Limits.* New York: Simon and Schuster, 1948.

Swinburne, Richard. *Faith and Reason.* Oxford: Clarendon Press, 2005.

———. *The Problems of Philosophy.* London: Oxford University Press, 1912.

van Frassen, Bas C. *The Empirical Stance.* New Haven, CT: Yale University, 2002.

van Huyssteen, J. Wentzel. *Essays in Postfoundationalist Theology.* Grand Rapids, MI: Eerdmans, 1997.

Wittgenstein, Ludwig. *On Certainty.* Edited by G. E. M. Anscombe and G. H. von Wright. Translated by Denis Paul and G. E. M. Anscombe. New York: Harper & Row, 1969.

———. *Tractatus Logico-Philosophicus.* 1921. Reprint, New York: Barnes & Noble, 2003.

Wood, W. Jay. *Epistemology: Becoming Intellectually Virtuous.* Downer's Grove, IL: Intervarsity Press, 1998.

INDEX